THE WOUND IN THE HEART

THE WOUND IN THE HEART

Michael Black

ARTHUR H. STOCKWELL LTD
Torrs Park   Ilfracombe   Devon
Established 1898
www.ahstockwell.co.uk

British Library Cataloguing-in-Publication Data.
A catalogue record for this book is available
from the British Library.

Arthur H. Stockwell Ltd bears no responsibility
for the accuracy of events recorded in this book.

ISBN 978-0-7223-3964-0
Printed in Great Britain by
Arthur H. Stockwell Ltd
Torrs Park   Ilfracombe
Devon

The Wound in the Heart

People are not always of the country in which they are born, and when you are prey to such a condition, you search everywhere for your true country.

Theophile Gautier

We shall find life tolerable once we have consented to be always ill at ease.

Gustave Flaubert

CHAPTER 1

For many years I've had a persistent dream of wandering alone through some large institution. The others there seem younger than me, and more successful. I return again and again, but get no nearer to finding out how I might graduate and move on. The people who run the place seem kindly disposed and do not throw me out. That comforts me, but my main feeling is of despair.

The dream seems to reflect not only part of my life; in a more profound way it sums up the whole of it. It is easy to see that the anxiety in this dream is related to the difficult years I spent in medical school – but, looked at in another way, I think it reflects my uneasy relationship with the world around me.

It is difficult to know where to begin, or what might interest anyone apart from me, and yet it seems a pity not to try to capture something of a life before it ends.

In some ways I'm a deeply conventional person. I am white, middle-class and, on the surface at least, have always believed that I should achieve a place in society. But there was a subtext that contradicted my conscious goals. Although on one hand I felt childishly omnipotent and that nothing should be beyond me, on the other I was hampered by a lack of confidence that has followed me into old age.

I was born in Ampthill in Bedfordshire in 1922, second son of Harry and Vera. My older brother was called Peter, and my younger sister was Jill. Harry, who had lost his right arm during the war, went off to the bank each day, leaving Vera and me together. Vera's mother died when she was four, and she was brought up by nuns as a boarder in a convent. Harry's father died when he was seven, and when these two met in the Great War neither could have been expected to know much about parenting.

Looking back, I speculate that Vera was looking for a lost mother in Harry, and he a lost father in his wife. What I'm more certain about is that Vera sought mothering from her children. I exclude Peter from this, because he somehow didn't fit into her scheme of relationships. But I was seen as more promising material. She was an immensely powerful, attractive woman and I loved her greatly, but I was also afraid of her.

Two sides of her stand out in memories from when I was perhaps four. She was weeping under a gas lamp in the Ampthill kitchen. I felt so sad and sorry but didn't know how to make her better. On another day we were invited to the Doctor's house, down the road in Flitwick. We had tea in the garden, and I behaved badly; Vera was mortified and hurried me along the path back to Ampthill, without speaking. I felt her rage because I had disgraced her. Vera often dealt with her anger towards me, throughout my growing-up, by withdrawing her love. It usually required efforts on my part to resume our close, if uncertain, relationship.

I loved and respected Harry, but I was unsure what he felt about me. I was called 'Little Mr Black' because of my supposed likeness to him. He barely features in my memories of Ampthill, and Peter is nowhere to be found. One affectionate memory I do have of my father is of sitting on his knee while he sang 'Ride a Cock Horse to Banbury Cross'.

I have two other powerful images of life in Ampthill. One is my first day at school. I am persuaded, reluctantly, to front the door of a dame school. The dame herself is dressed all in black and wears a long skirt. She's critical and unkind. This memory is quite possibly false, but it stays with me. The second, however, is authentic, and at this point I need to give some family history.

Vera's father, Montague, was a lawyer in Bedfordshire. He married Alice and they had two children, Curzon and Vera. When Alice died Montague was grief-stricken and one can only imagine what it was like for him with two young children. One clue may be that when I accompanied Vera, in her old age and after many years' absence, on a visit to her mother's grave in a large cemetery, she led me to the spot and dug away with bare hands until the overgrown gravestone reappeared. This suggested that she must have spent many unhappy hours there with her mother.

Montague Austin had a maid called Annie, and after Alice's death Annie occupied a more exalted position in the household. She became the housekeeper, and she entered Montague's bed and eventually married him. Vera was deeply attached to her father and jealous of Annie; she resented Annie's becoming mistress of the house. And so she was sent away to the nuns at a young age. She told me once that she would have never left Montague to get married if he had been on his own.

Annie (Granny Austin) I can never quite place, because Harry's mother (Granny Black) seemed to be my real grandmother. My only clear recollection of Annie was of her coming to stay in our Ampthill house. During her visit there was a dramatic scene between the two women. I have no idea what it was about, but clearly there was a fierce row between them. After a crescendo, Annie, bags packed, hurried down the stairs, out of the front door and out of our lives. She was never seen again. I was probably five years old, and I was unable to understand what had happened, but it must have reinforced my opinion that Vera was such a powerful woman that she could even make her stepmother disappear for ever. Clearly my mother was not to be trifled with.

Our house moves followed Harry's promotions in the Westminster Bank. He was a diligent and able man and by degrees we moved along the London, Midland and Scottish railway.

Our first stop after Ampthill was St Albans, when I was five. I was enrolled in a small school run by Miss Kidd in her home. She was a nice, hearty, religious woman and she lived with her father, a retired missionary. One day we heard that Mr Kidd had died. His daughter could be heard crying in the outside lavatory. I was ignorant of grief and thought it a huge joke. I shared a bedroom with Peter and told him of Miss Kidd's behaviour with amusement.

On Fridays Vera took Peter and me to Lyons' for lunch, and we always chose fish and chips. One day a young man shared our table. We all got on well, and when he was leaving he said he would like to see Peter and me again. Vera was obviously not going to agree, and when we got home she explained that "There were some men . . ." I cannot remember how she put it, but this was my first introduction to the idea that a man might be sexually attracted to a boy.

When I was six I developed scarlet fever. In those days it was a serious illness, and I was admitted to the fever hospital for six weeks. I'd never been separated from my family before, and I felt quite lost. Visitors were not allowed, but I remember Vera standing outside the window showing me an egg which she had brought for me. I also have a memory that the nurse in charge was an unpleasant, unfeeling woman – but again this may be my distorted recollection of a woman in authority.

The other children on the ward found my accent odd, and one girl asked me, "Does the puddin ding?" and I was generally teased. The food was unpleasant and the stew disgusting, but at the end of my time there things improved. Spring arrived and we soaked our feet in bowls of water to get rid of the shedding skin before going home.

When I arrived, so happy to be back, Vera wasted little time before arousing my guilt; "Haven't you noticed something different?" she said.

It turned out that our dog, Bengy, had been run over and killed and I'd not even noticed. Later Vera told me that she'd been distressed by sending me away, but the Doctor had told her that the only way that I could be kept at home would be to hang a sheet soaked in disinfectant at the top of the stairs, and this she felt unable to do.

For some time after this separation I became phobic about leaving the house. Vera tried to take me to school, but after a few yards I'd break away and run home. I was not the only one with emotional problems. Vera became depressed and the Doctor said that she needed "to be taken out of herself". She joined the local amateur dramatics society and was cast in the role of a country girl in an Edwardian opera. This was in the late 1920s, when more modern musicals were on the way, so this was quite an old-fashioned affair.

Vera embarked on a flirtatious relationship with one of the boys in the cast and soon cheered up. The main character, Nan, was played by a somewhat overweight lady with a good singing voice. The *pièce de résistance* was a song called 'Under the Deodar' and there were parts for two blacked-up boys in the cast. Peter was selected, but I was considered too young. This annoyed me greatly because I was certain I'd have put him in the shade.

Although I lacked confidence in other ways, I seem to have had no doubt about my star potential!

Vera and I both improved emotionally. Granny Black came to stay, having driven her Rover car from Scotland. In those days cars were uncommon and women drivers even more so. We planned to drive back with her to the Clyde, where she had a bungalow, and it had been arranged that we would stop for the night on the way. On the morning of leaving, everything was ready, except that her driving cushion could not be found. I had in fact hidden it, and there was great commotion. Looking back at my young self, I'm amazed at my cheek and ability to carry it off. I think that by this time my self-confidence must have been wavering, and perhaps this defiance was its last full flurry.

CHAPTER 2

In 1930 we moved to Mill Hill in North West London, because my father had been made manager of the Finchley Road branch of the bank. It was a comfortable four-bedroom suburban house with a large back garden. It cost £1,000. Peter was enrolled at Haberdashers' Aske's school in Cricklewood, and I went to a preparatory school for boys, Highwood. I think that by then I was in a certain amount of emotional trouble, although I was still able to learn.

Socially I was not a great success. Indeed, I can remember at a low point some of the other boys marching round the garden singing 'We've Got to Get Rid of the Rats', and I was one of the rats. I also felt confused sexually. I had been to see a then popular children's patriotic play called *Where the Rainbow Ends* and was greatly impressed by the two dashing youths who stood up to evil until, at the end, St George arrived and the children were reunited with their parents. But there were also *girls* involved and I can remember one lesson, when we were all sitting on the floor in the room, I was fantasising about whether the girls in the play had put powder on their somewhat hazy genitalia.

However, these fantasies faded when I met my friend Coombe. He was younger than me, also unpopular, and in some respects I looked after him. For example, we were chosen to fight together in a boxing match. I was the stronger, but I deliberately held back. As a result we were awarded half a point each, and this made me feel aggrieved.

I don't remember how it first came about, but we soon became sexual friends. There was a large old-fashioned lavatory on the first floor of the school, and Coombe and I went in there after making sure that no one had seen us. Coombe wore little blue trousers with buttons at the side. I was the instigator, and I would unbutton these in order to see his erect penis. I think that this was probably the most thrilling sexual encounter that I've ever had. After a few minutes one of us would start buttoning himself up again and we would leave separately. We became bolder: we made holes in our trouser pockets and fondled one another in class until the headmaster told us to stop. Undeterred, we did the same thing in the playground, telling the other boys that we were "examining our treasures". Surprisingly they seemed to find our behaviour amusing and made no attempt to stop it.

Of course this idyll came to an end. I asked my mother if Coombe could stay for the weekend, no doubt imagining a night of illicit pleasure, but then guilt overcame me and I confessed all. She seemed quite sanguine about it, telling me not to do it again, and I think that she implied that my father would be excluded from our secret. I suppose I had to drop Coombe after this, although I don't really remember. What I do recall, however, with some shame, is my last recollection of my first lover; he was in the school garden surrounded by jeering boys, and, as I remember, his trousers were down and his penis was erect. I did nothing to help him.

The school was run by a Mr Seaton. I thought him on the whole kindly, but I was still afraid of him. He had a sickly wife, for whom no diagnosis seemed to fit, and one young son. I had been intrigued to read that the female star of a popular film called *Trader Horn* had succumbed to a tropical illness, and I wondered if the same fate had befallen Mrs Seaton. Of the teachers I remember, Mr Mawson, a dashing figure with a moustache, behaved gallantly towards Mrs Ferguson, mother of one of the pupils, and I thought he lusted after her. I preferred another master, Mr Moffatt, who would appear in the mornings with shaving cream sticking to his ears. He made it clear he was on the side of the boys, rather than authority.

Mr Moffatt, some other boys and I met after school to rehearse a play he wanted to produce. We also visited him at his flat one day. Again this play didn't come to anything; this may have been connected with the fact that he became more openly subversive and began to criticise Mr Seaton to us. Eventually we decided that he should not be doing this, and we reported him to the headmaster. The errant teacher was instantly dismissed. It seems a strange thing for us to have done, but I suppose his dislike of authority was too great for us to feel comfortable about.

The only woman on the staff was the art teacher, Miss Heatherington. She tried hard with me, discussing perspective, the use of paint and making linocuts, but I had no aptitude. I must have been a sad disappointment to her.

A family called the Pearces lived opposite. We thought them common and *nouveau riche*, but they had a car and the two boys were driven to Highwood each morning. The school was some distance away and up a hill, and at that time there was no bus, so I timed my exit from our house so that the Pearces would pick us up. It must have been obvious what we were doing, and yet neither family suggested making a regular commitment. When there was no lift, Vera would take me to school in the morning and I would come home again at lunchtime, in a crocodile of little boys. After lunch Vera presumably took me back to school.

When I was older I went on my own to school. An old woman tramp whom we called Mary lived in a shack in the fields by the road. We schoolboys thought she was a witch and threw stones at her whenever she was sighted; she would then swear at us.

Although friends were a difficulty, there was a boy called Fisher who wanted to be my blood brother and produced a penknife so that we could seal our fraternity in blood. I refused, and this probably cooled or ended the relationship. Part of my difficulty in being accepted was that I was not much interested in boyish things and was hopeless at games – sports afternoons, whether summer or winter, were something to be endured. We played cricket and football, and I don't know which caused me more anxiety.

During my last years at the school, Mr Seaton said he would like me to be a prefect, but the only problem was that I was still in the second cricket team. "Would you mind this arrangement?" he asked. I said no; I was pleased to be recognised as a prefect, but I also felt humiliated.

There were two brothers at the school called Musson 1 and Musson 2. One day they did not arrive and we were told (I don't remember how) that Mr Musson had gassed himself. The two boys came back the next day, and they were obviously upset. I noticed that one of the brothers' breath smelt, which I associated with his grief. I'm fairly sure that none of us said anything to the boys to indicate our shock or concern.

CHAPTER 3

When I was thirteen I had to leave Highwood and go to a senior school. My parents decided on University College School (UCS) in Hampstead, although they had sent Peter to Haberdashers' Aske's. I thought this was favouritism to me, and I had an idea that I was supposed to be the bright one of the family. If this was the case, they were to be sadly disappointed. I had to sit an entrance exam and one of the exercises was to describe my best friend. I was at a loss since I did not have one, so I wrote about a boy called Donald Pearson, whom I met only once a year. He was the son of neighbours in Ampthill, and his mother was suspected as having 'a touch of the tar brush'. When we moved to Mill Hill, they came to stay each year for the Hendon Air Pageant; in those days this was a spectacular event and we took a picnic to the park, from where we watched the display.

I don't think I got on particularly well with Donald. One year, when Peter was away, Donald and I shared the bedroom. I suppose he must have invited me because I climbed into his bed, and he grasped me very tightly, saying nothing. I never understood what he really wanted, although it was obviously some kind of sexual advance and perhaps a desire to show his power over me. But it went no further and I'm sure we never discussed it.

I started at UCS in September 1936. By then I had become friendly with a boy called Geoffrey Ellis, who lived in the next road. He was rather plump, as I was, and also somehow out of the mainstream of boyish things. His mother was called Winnie – someone with whom in later years I had a rather flirtatious relationship – but he had no father. Mr Ellis was never mentioned, but somehow we discovered that he had a mental breakdown and was an inpatient in a psychiatric hospital.

Geoffrey and I used to travel to school together, which meant catching the No. 113 bus to Hendon Central and the Underground to Hampstead. I wish I could remember what Hampstead looked like in those days, but I cannot. We walked along Church Row, cutting through the private road where we told ourselves that Gracie Fields lived, and then down Frognal. One thing I do remember, however, is seeing a flickering television screen in Drazin's shop window.

I cannot remember much about the first year at UCS, but I must have kept my head above water because in the second year I was moved into the more academically rigorous fourth form. Here I was faced with studying maths, physics and chemistry with a Mr Stanley. He was a popular master, but for some reason I became his victim. I had no talent anyway for any of his subjects, but when he spoke directly to me any wits which I did have disappeared. As I remember, he had piercing eyes and bushy white hair and pointed out my incomprehension in front of the class as if he were using a scalpel. Many years later I heard that he had died, and I was delighted!

On another occasion I was kept behind by a normally mild master to complete some sums. I could not do them, and eventually he cried despairingly, "Are you mad, boy?" I was getting on so badly that my father was sent for. Nobody seemed to realise how unhappy and disturbed I was at this time (in the late 1930s), and the result of the discussion was that I was to be given a half-term report as well as the usual one.

Another agony for me was twice-weekly games, on Tuesdays and Thursdays, and also physical training (PT). I think I must have played rugby during the first winter term, though I always managed to avoid cricket. In order to get out of games, one had to take a note to the headmaster. My mother was often willing to write that I had a cold or sore throat; then I would wait outside Mr Walton's door. He always seemed pleased to see me, and amused that I would bring yet another letter. One day, however, he suggested benignly that I should sometimes try to play games.

We travelled twice a week from Finchley Road to Richmond on the Broad Street line, for boating. We banked, however, on the fact that sometimes the river was unsuitable for our boats, and we waited at lunchtime for a notice on the board to say whether or not we had to go. We rejoiced on the days rain cancelled the trip and we went home early.

PT was another obstacle to be overcome. I could not climb ropes or vault horses, and I approached each session with much anxiety. This was not helped by the fact that the boys I most admired could climb and vault with ease.

My two favourites were Jackson and Fraser, neither of whom acknowledged my existence. Fraser called Jackson 'Jacko', and they walked around with one arm swung casually round the other's shoulder, each calling the other 'man'. They did not know that I used to discreetly peer at their naked bodies when we were showering after PT. I eventually managed to get out of PT as well as games by joining the Garden Club. I had a small plot within the school grounds, and I would thankfully escape there, although I was not much of a gardener.

I struggled through the fourth year and entered the fifth. By then it must have been clear that I was no good at science, and I was put into an easier class with, thankfully, no Mr Stanley. Our form master was Mr Burrows, whom we nicknamed Bertie. He taught us history and was variable in temper: when he was in a good mood he was amusing and friendly, but on other days he was strict and distant in manner. Most of the boys could not distinguish which Mr Burrows had joined us in the mornings, and they would joke with the wrong one. However, my instincts, trained at home to pick up the nuances of my mother's moods, knew immediately, and I thought my classmates obtuse.

I began to enjoy the fifth year. I now felt more at home with other boys. This didn't, however, include Laurie – he was a fat boy, the son of Lupino Lane, who was then a well-known stage and film actor. Laurie was often absent because he was also an actor. One day, however, he said to me witheringly, "You'll never be a prefect." I console myself now by knowing that neither would he – nor a famous actor!

As the year went on we began to prepare for the School Certificate exams. In those days you could pass in different subjects, and if you got five credits this was equivalent to matriculation. Although I felt more settled, I still found it hard to study and to learn. In the summer of 1939 we sat the exams, and

I still have the papers somewhere. I passed in three subjects – English, French and one other – but I think I got no credits. After the exams we relaxed and there was talk of going into the sixth form. I remember sitting in the school garden with another boy and actually having a sensible conversation with him. He told me his parents were going to see *Tonight at 8.30* by Noel Coward. It seemed to me that next year I would begin to fit into this new world, and we agreed to meet again.

CHAPTER 4

By 1939 Germany had taken Austria, and then the rest of Czechoslovakia. My parents were obviously afraid of another war so soon, twenty years after the last one. Although we observed the two-minutes' silence at school, the Great War seemed very far away, especially as my father never mentioned it. Neville Chamberlain, the prime minister, met Hitler in Munich and said it was 'peace in our time'. My mother wrote to him, recommending some kind of tonic – a pick-me-up to give him strength.

When my exam results arrived we opened them in the kitchen, and both my parents were obviously disappointed in their 'clever' son. I was disappointed too, although I had not expected anything better.

We went to the Isle of Wight for our summer holiday that year – Vera, Harry, Jill and I. Peter was with his Territorial Army regiment; he had joined the Honourable Artillery Company, which we thought very grand. We stayed on a farm and the weather was sunny; the farmhands were gathering the harvest, and Vera, Jill and I joined in. Vera was in her element and rode on top of the hay cart with several lusty young men as escorts. It was too good to last. One night after Harry had gone back to London and we had gone to bed, I heard a curious moaning coming from Vera's room. "Where am I?" she kept repeating in a curious, monotonous voice. Jill and I stayed with her. I was sixteen and felt both frightened and responsible for this strange new mother.

In the morning I telephoned Harry, who arrived the next day, and we all went home by car. Vera was still in the same state, and she stayed in it for some time after we got back. No doubt the Doctor was called, but I don't know what he diagnosed. I imagine that he was as puzzled as we were. Years later, when I was studying psychiatry, I realised she had been suffering from hysterical fugues.

She went on having these into old age, and she was terrified of them – although they also had their uses. (After Harry died I stayed with her for several days; on the day that I was due to go back to work she begged me to stay, saying that she feared one of her 'blackouts' was coming on. I explained that I had no choice but to leave her, and the fugue did not appear.)

During the summer of 1939, I started having wet dreams. I did not know what these were, and I was dismayed by this emerging white fluid. I told Vera, not Harry, of what was happening. She said that I was "not to worry" and that it came "from somewhere else". This was my only sex education. My genitals began to develop pleasurable sensations and I told Peter this; he said it was wrong to rub myself and that I should not do so. However, the temptations were too strong and I found out for myself how the white fluid was produced. After the first time I vowed never to do it again, but alas! my resolve often weakened, although my feelings of guilt remained strong.

CHAPTER 5

By late summer it was obvious we were going to war with Germany. I was expected to go back to school, and I was jolted when Harry told me that I was to leave and go into the local branch of the Westminster Bank as a junior clerk. He gave us the reason that the journey from Mill Hill to Hampstead would be uncertain in wartime. But the real reason was that I would be a companion to Vera, since the bank was only a few minutes' walk from our house.

I did not resist this plan, and I now find it difficult to understand how I could have been so supine. Several boys whom I was just beginning to relate to went on into the sixth form, and I felt the odd one out. There were three of us at the bank: Mr Jenner (the manager), Mr Hatfield (the chief clerk) and me. There were big ledgers, and virtually everything was done by hand. I started with the simple tasks, but I was soon promoted to cashier. This was all for twenty-five shillings per week, less nine old pence in insurance. I gave my mother ten shillings a week and opened a Post Office savings account. I enjoyed talking to the customers and became good at my job. However, it was never my intention to make my career in banking, and although Harry arranged for me to do a postal course to gain banking qualifications I never really followed this.

The war started and I joined the Local Defence Volunteers, which later became the Home Guard. I was a messenger, and I rode around Mill Hill at night delivering messages on my bicycle (what on earth was in them, I wonder?). We practised running towards sandbags and stabbing them with bayonets, shouting at them as though they were Germans.

I kept up contact with a boy who was still at school, and we went for walks in the park in the evening. He was a good-looking fifteen-year-old, and I was greatly attracted to him, although I would not have admitted this to myself at the time. He seemed not to feel guilty about masturbation (wanking) and he speculated how many times he had done it ("I hope not more than a hundred times"). He had a friend who was an even greater exponent of this delight. I was fascinated by this sexual talk, but it did not lessen my own feelings of guilt.

Margaret was my own particular girlfriend; we shared an interest in cinema and theatre and were close. There was, however, a problem: she lived in the next road, and when I left her at her house I always felt I ought to kiss her but never did so. At the time I thought it was shyness, but it was also of course because I was not attracted to women.

During the winter of 1940/1, she and I thought that our lives needed brightening up. We decided to hold a dance, and we set about planning this. We booked the hall of the local parish school, arranged refreshments – sandwiches, cakes and soft drinks – and discussed whom to invite. It was sixty years ago, and in my memory it's like the Duvivier film *Un Carnet de Bal*. I expect the hall was really quite small, and the event not as exciting as my memory dictates, but it remains for ever with me.

The invitation list included some boys from UCS: Malcolm, Margaret's brother, Jackson (Jacko) and others. The girls included June, my cousin. She had become a startlingly pretty seventeen-year-old, and she arrived in a dress which she'd made herself. The evening was a great success. Geoffrey played the piano and there was no question at that stage of our lives of serving (or missing) alcohol. There was much discussion as to which guest would sleep in which house. June obviously would stay with us. I was also hoping that Jacko would stay, but he was captured by A. G., who was thought by some of her peers (including me) to be the local tart. I settled for Peter Tuch, a refugee from Nazi Germany, whom I did not know very well and who had impeccable manners.

Because of the war Harry and Vera turned our dining room into an air-raid shelter with sandbagged windows and wooden supports for the ceiling. Different parts of the room were curtained off, and when the siren sounded neighbours arrived in various states of dress. The air raids were severe, but after a time we became blasé and I used to stay in my bedroom. There were some tragedies and excitements, though. The young daughter of the local newsagent was killed by a bomb, and a British aeroplane crashed into the house next door to Margaret's and the pilot was killed. My friend Ron Allen joined up as an RAF navigator and was later killed in action.

During the Blitz, Peter and I went to a concert at the then Queen's Hall near Oxford Circus on the night of the greatest wartime bombing raid on London. There was no public transport and, as he and I walked home to Mill Hill, one particularly heavy bomb exploded. I panicked and fell down on the pavement; he remained upright and showed more courage than me.

CHAPTER 6

By early 1941 I was tired of the bank and also of living in Mill Hill. I'd become friendly with Neville Davis, and we used to meet for coffee on Saturday mornings. He used to tell me about each new, wonderful girl whom he had met, but these liaisons never seemed to get anywhere. Neville was also tired of his present life, and we suddenly decided to join the navy. My decision was greatly influenced by two things. On a recent visit to Scotland to see relatives, I had met on the night train a sailor who had greatly impressed me. I can't remember now what we talked about, but no doubt he told me stories about his profession. The other influence on my decision was the fact that Peter was a lieutenant in the army, and my rivalry meant that I wanted to join a different service.

Neville and I went together to the recruitment centre in Burnt Oak. By then we were both eighteen, and, slightly to my surprise, the recruiting officer took us seriously. He told us that there were vacancies for stokers or for ordinary seamen. We thought that the stoking sounded too much like hard work and settled for being ordinary seamen (not that we had any idea of what we would have to do). I went home and told my parents what I'd done; they seemed to be delighted.

In June of 1941 the summons came. Neville and I were to report to HMS *Raleigh* in Torpoint, Cornwall. He and I must have travelled separately, because Harry and Vera went to the station to see me off on my own. When we got there I realised that I'd forgotten my gas mask. Harry went back on the Underground to fetch it. Eventually I was on the train and ready to say goodbye; no doubt Vera kissed me, but what I have remembered ever since is Harry through the open window kissing me goodbye. This was one of the most important moments of my life.

At HMS *Raleigh* we were issued with uniforms and assorted kit. One of my first memories is of seeing unlimited chocolate on sale. Life was going to be very different from Mill Hill. A less happy memory is of endless square-bashing in the hot sun without proper protection. I developed quite severe burns on my shoulders and had to have treatment.

I made new friends, including Dave, a slightly effete man with a drawly accent. Dave had another friend, and Neville and I went with them to a local fair. I sat on the friend's knee on the roundabout. "What a pity you are not a little boy," he said. These were new levels of sophistication for me. On another evening we went on the ferry and into Plymouth for a meal. Plymouth had suffered a severe air bombardment and we were recruited to help bombed householders sort out their possessions. We helped one such woman, who gave us half a crown for our trouble, and we spent it on the pictures.

On that evening in Plymouth we passed a local pub. I realised it was full of 'queers', who were talking in a sibilant, stereotyped way to one another. I was full of prejudice and disgust at such behaviour.

After twelve weeks we moved to HMS *Drake*, another naval land establishment. I have a few random memories: a Cockney man reaching over the table and removing some of my meal with his fork. "You don't want that, mate, do you?" he asked. He also talked of missing his wife: "the old sexual intercourse". We went to the base cinema and saw Joan Crawford in *Susan and God*. During one particularly dramatic entrance down a flight of stairs, one rating shouted, "Look out, missus, you'll get fucked!"

In the mornings we washed and shaved in metal basins arranged so that each one had a twin on the opposite side. One morning I looked up and saw Michael Redgrave opposite me. I was too shy to speak to him, although, as an attractive eighteen-year-old, he might have welcomed my overture.

My main memory is of the gunnery school, which was run by tough, bullying senior ratings. The course lasted for six weeks, during which we were supposed to learn about the innards of various guns as well as doing more parade-ground drill. After a time this was more than I could manage, and I developed difficulty in swallowing. I was admitted to the sickbay, where a perceptive doctor prescribed a week's sick leave.

Much later in life I realised I'd developed a psychiatric condition called globus hystericus, and as soon as I got home it cleared up. I can't remember anything about going back, but I must have finished the course. However, my week's absence put me behind my friends, and Neville and others were drafted to ships while I waited for my own draft ship. I was told to report to HMS *Trinidad*, a new cruiser which had just been completed in Plymouth Dockyard. Our living space was at the fore of the ship, and consisted of a table (one of a number on the mess deck where about ten of us ate) and various spaces with hooks in the bulkhead, where we slung our hammocks. Our hammocks were valued possessions and were guarded carefully. I slung mine over an open trapdoor, and this taught me how to make sure that my knots were correctly tied.

At first my messmates were suspicious of me, and I must have seemed a curious creature – young, nervous, and with a posh accent. In fact, one of them said at one point, "Does your mother know you're out?" After some time, however, by doing more than my fair share of chores, and because they realised how innocent I was, they accepted me as another mate. Throughout the mess deck, a group of us had already been noticed as potential officer material before beginning our training, and we soon, though I can't remember now how, knew about one another and banded together. Our group was not popular on the lower deck, although we were careful not to give ourselves airs and graces. "A bunch of brown-hatters" was how one rating summed us up.

Although the lower deck had a reputation for homosexuality, I did not see much evidence of this. There was obviously a homosexual culture in the lower deck, though, and many ratings had a 'winger'. This was a younger man with whom he shared an emotional, though not necessarily a sexual, relationship. There was one young regular rating, however, who, even in my innocence, I believed gave his sexual favours. He had dyed blonde hair and was called, unsurprisingly, 'Blondie' by his mates. During his time on the *Trinidad*, however, he seemed to change. He stopped dying his hair, and I suspect that his favours also stopped.

I had my share of offers, as a school friend of Vera's used to say; the most memorable was from a leading seaman. He, his mates and I were travelling in the lift when the lights went out. I was given a powerful kiss before the lights shone again. The leading seaman and his mates laughed at me, and I'm sure that he'd been dared to do it. I was angry and upset, but if I'd reacted favourably I might have become his winger.

While we were still in Plymouth, however, the main activity was heterosexual. One member of our mess deck – an endearing and not very bright man – went ashore, got drunk and picked up a prostitute. When he arrived back we all crowded round as he pulled out his penis, laid it on the table and told us proudly that he had come six times. We believed him, and I was both excited and awestricken.

After sea trials we left Plymouth Harbour and the Captain announced that we were sailing to Scapa Flow. After more trials we headed for Iceland, where we went ashore and got drunk in the NAAFI. Then we were told we were to escort a convoy of merchant ships taking supplies to Murmansk. It was December and breathtakingly cold; we could not touch metal with our bare hands because of burning.

I became a member of the 4-inch-gun crew. We worked in watches, four hours on, four hours off, and of course we had to man the gun when 'action stations' sounded. I was made communications rating, and I relayed messages from the gunnery officer on the bridge to the gun captain, Petty Officer Southan. I suspect that I was chosen both because I was intelligent and because I was not strong enough in the arms to load the heavy ammunition into the gun. But there was a drawback: while the other crew members wore earplugs, I couldn't (for obvious reasons). Later in life this was to contribute to some of my high-tone deafness.

While we were in port we could wash and shower in a spacious washroom. Once at sea, however, this came to an end and our ablutions became quite rudimentary. I shared a bucket with several others, all using the same water to wash our faces. I don't remember about shaving, but probably we didn't. Petty Officer Southan, the captain of the gun crew, was a kind, friendly man who gossiped with us while we drank Kye, a very strong drink made out of naval chocolate.

We steamed along the Arctic route in the company of destroyers and other ships, escorting the merchant navy vessels. There were a number of alarms, and a good many 'action stations', but no real encounter with the enemy. It was an eerie journey, as it took place mainly in the dark with only a few hours of gloomy daylight.

Before we reached Murmansk there was a more serious threat of enemy action, probably from submarines. The Captain decided to increase speed. We left the convoy and didn't stop until we reached the anchorage for Murmansk. I thought it was rather unsporting to leave the convoy in this way, but I guess it was decided not to risk this new and expensive ship at that time.

CHAPTER 7

On leaving the *Trinidad*, it was Scapa Flow again. We travelled back from Scotland by train and I decided to break our journey overnight with Vera and Harry. I filled my matelot cap with bars of chocolate and emptied them with a flourish. I was grimy and thin in the face, and with affection I turned the familiar geyser on for a hot bath.

The next morning I met my companions and we travelled to Plymouth. We had been expected the previous evening, and we were told off for staying in London, but there was no other punishment and we were sent on indefinite leave. Indefinite leave was a curious feature of my naval life. I never knew how long it would last, and, since Vera brought me breakfast in bed, I was always waiting for her to bring up the dreaded envelope. On this first occasion I was summoned to HMS *King Alfred*. This consisted of two shore bases, the first a former school, Lancing College, and the second a converted swimming bath on Brighton seafront.

The summons was in order for the authorities to decide if I was a suitable candidate for officer training. I was given digs with a Mrs Helme and her daughter Mary. Mary was older than me, and the war supplied her with a succession of young men with whom she could exercise her charms.

On the day I was to be interviewed, mother and daughter wished me luck and I set off nervously for the interview. There were two or three senior officers sitting at a table with me opposite them. They produced two models of ships and asked me how they should pass each other; the correct answer was that they should pass each other on the starboard side. I gave the wrong answer and they sent me outside to wait for their decision. When they called me back they said that they realised that I'd been very nervous and they announced that I'd been accepted.

At that time each weekly intake was of one hundred ratings, and so perhaps my acceptance to become an officer was not so surprising. I think that my posh accent (thanks to Vera) helped. We were transferred to Brighton and, as a parting present, I promised that when I became an officer Mary would have my matelot trousers. She had asked for these and was delighted. Vera was less so and made her view clear.

I was again supplied with digs in Brighton, but Vera had already made other arrangements for me. She had an old friend, a nurse, who lived with her partner, another nurse. Vera hinted darkly at their relationship, saying that her partner was jealous of her. I noted that they shared a bedroom – whatever that meant. They were both extremely kind to me, and their flat was a haven after the former swimming baths.

My memories of my time in Brighton are a mixture of fairly incomprehensible lessons in navigation and other unknown subjects, and much drilling – only this time I had to act as the one in command. Somehow I got through it all, although I achieved low pass marks in the final exam. I tried not to mind, and went to Gieves' to be fitted for my midshipman's uniform. The tailor was a Mr Blowes, father of Beryl, whom I was to meet a year later as a Wren officer in Southampton. I went home on leave in my uniform with its two red tabs, much to Vera and Harry's admiration. I was aware that when I walked down the street people looked at me, much to my pleasure.

From 1942 to '43 I had a succession of postings in what was called Combined Operations. We were being trained as boat officers and I met some old friends again, notably Chick and Dave, although in fact Dave was by now fairly hostile towards me.

One such posting was to a former holiday camp in Brightlingsea, and the final one was to Scotland. During the day we exercised from a large house on the mainland, and when off duty we lived in another large house on the isle of Shona, on the west coast. We were a group of young men and there were no women – apart from Flora and her colleague, who ran the house. We often thought about and talked about sex. I was still extremely reticent and felt guilty about this subject, but many of the others talked quite freely about their experiences, which seemed to be mainly about masturbation. I shared a room with a Scottish Royal Marine who wore a kilt. I hadn't undressed one evening when he told me he had fucked innumerable women and was now starting on men. He eyed my eighteen-year-old frame and said that I was just what he liked. Needless to say, I rebuffed him.

Another suitor was F., who invited me to share his room. He entertained us by describing a 'wanking machine' he had made. This consisted of Meccano to which were attached rotating feathers.

We were now supposed to be ready for action. One day we were doing an exercise when the commander in charge pointed at my landing craft, because I was obviously doing something wrong. I was mortified when the other young officer in the craft explained that we were now 'trained boat officers'.

Sometimes a signal would arrive saying that different postings were available; one such was as a Russian interpreter. It's a measure of my desperation that I applied, having only three pass marks in School Certificate and no knowledge of Russian. Another more fruitful application was for two officers to apply for the job of advanced gunnery-training officers. Another young man and I applied and both were accepted, although I think now that they were perhaps glad to get rid of us.

Looking back at my young self, I'm amazed at my lack of self-knowledge. It should have been obvious to me that I was ill suited to being a naval officer, and that given my experiences at the gunnery school it was madness to think that I could become a gunnery officer. However, it's clear that I had no such insight, and I arrived at HMS *Squid* in Southampton, having been promoted to acting temporary lieutenant RNVR with two stripes of wavy gold braid.

HMS *Squid* was a block of flats which had been requisitioned for the war. The officer in charge of my unit was Commander Ryder, VC, commonly known as Red Ryder. He'd been decorated for a daring although unsuccessful raid on St Nazaire, and I found his cold, reticent manner extremely formidable. Second in command was Lieutenant Hotham, a much more sympathetic figure. His secretary was Beryl Blowes, whose father had supplied my uniform in Brighton. She was a warm, sweet girl and we became friends.

Soon after I arrived, the unit set out on a trial expedition with Commander Ryder in the leading landing craft. As a gunnery officer I was supposed to accompany him, but they set off without me. This did not get me off to a good start. On a later trial one of the Oerliken guns jammed; I was expected to free it but couldn't do so. Commander Ryder then summoned the signals officer, who managed to get it working again. I felt humiliated.

After some time, Beryl asked me to go to her office. With embarrassment she gave me my confidential report. This was extremely critical. I cannot remember the wording but my self-esteem plummeted further. At some point I explained that I'd only been trained in small arms (not that I was any good with these), and an additional gunnery officer was sent for. A Royal Marines officer, Lieutenant Fisher, arrived and to my relief turned out to be well disposed towards me. He was later replaced by Captain Payton Jones, an extremely amiable man who didn't seem dismayed by my deficiencies.

The person who raised my sagging self-esteem was a naval doctor who also lived on the base (although he wasn't connected to my unit). This was Lieutenant Roderick Ross, who to my surprise took an interest in me. He was Canadian and recently married to Anne, who remained in Canada. He was extremely good-looking and very popular. Quite soon he made it clear that he would like me to go to the cinema with him instead of another officer. Until then I usually spent the evenings with Beryl and her friends, in their quarters, but with Rod I developed a different pattern.

Several of us would go into Southampton and cruise the pubs. Alcohol of any sort was scarce but could be found by determined young men. To my shame I remember that on one evening we spied a table with several full glasses, which we quickly emptied. The indignant owners came back and we had no excuse. I began to smoke Canadian cigarettes called C2C, nicknamed 'Camel to Consumer'.

My troubles with Commander Ryder were not, however, over. He called me in one day because some small-arms spare parts had not arrived. "Black," he said, "I want these spare parts. Go and find them and don't come back until you have done so" (or some such). This was in September 1943, and my twenty-first birthday was on the 27th. I telephoned the war office and made an appointment, and so spent my birthday walking the corridors pleading, I suppose, for this absent machinery. I must have been successful because some time later the missing parts turned up at a gunnery store, but I don't think that this made Red think any the better of me.

As gunnery officer it was my job to drill the ratings. An officer of the Wrens – a formidable lady called Mrs Butters – asked me to train her recruits. By then I'd become accustomed to squad drill and was quite good at it. As I put these girls through their paces, Mrs Butters looked on approvingly.

A much more daunting job was to come next – Admiral Louis Mountbatten, chief of Combined Operations, decided to visit Southampton in order to give a pep talk to the troops. He was to be received in an enormous shed in the docks, and my men and I were responsible for welcoming him with a naval salute, ending with a 'present arms'. We rehearsed meticulously, marching in formation till we reached the office door through which Mountbatten would arrive. Unfortunately it did not work out as we had hoped; while we waited expectantly there was suddenly a loud banging at a door on the other side of the shed. It opened to reveal the great man with suitable gold-braided escort. I had the presence of mind to retrieve the situation, however, and we marched to our new position and gave our salute. Mountbatten quickly told us to fall out and to gather round. I don't remember what he said, but he radiated a sense of comradeship and a feeling that we were all in this together.

Beryl was thoroughly overworked, and I think she had her own problems with Commander Ryder. She became ill, and eventually her legs refused to work and she could no longer function. She collapsed with an hysterical paralysis, and she was sent on leave. She completely recovered and we all treated her with more care and consideration afterwards. For some reason Lieutenant Hotham took on the running of the unit. Beryl again gave me my confidential report – this time much kinder in tone, although not altogether uncritical.

The months went by and, with Rod's support and in the absence of Commander Ryder, I began to enjoy myself. I've often thought about the nature of our relationship. Looking back, for my part it's clear that I basked in the approval of an older man; I speculate that as a heterosexual with a new young wife he wanted a non-sexual companion. I was an attractive, quite feminine younger man and we each gave the other what he needed at the time.

CHAPTER 8

In the early months of 1944 it was clear that there was something in the wind. Landing-craft exercises and trials continued and I took part in these. In early June we transferred to Cowes on the Isle of Wight. Rod came over from the mainland and we had tea in a café. I think we both realised that we would not be meeting again for some time, if at all.

On 4 June, we assembled and were ready to sail; then there was a postponement for twenty-four hours and we finally set off for Normandy on the evening of 5 June. I don't need to go into too much detail about the postponement – of course, this is already widely known. Briefly, the weather forecast for the Channel was bad, but a lull was detected and General Eisenhower, commander of the invasion troops, decided to go ahead. I travelled on the deck of a LCI (landing craft infantry) and my job was to be one of a team co-ordinating one section of the troop landings. It was an extraordinary feeling as we travelled through the night. I don't think that I was particularly nervous; the whole episode seemed too extraordinary and unreal. As we approached the French coast we saw an unbelievable sight. Waves of bombers flew overhead and huge numbers of rockets were fired from special landing craft. The sea was full of ships – both landing craft, full of troops, and their naval escorts.

We were assigned to one of the British beaches, code-named Juno, and we took up our position offshore. For the next thirty-six hours we worked without sleep, directing our section of craft with loudhailers. We watched the landing craft disgorge their men on to the beach and the DUKWs driving up to the beach and then continuing on to the shore and beyond. I was full of admiration for the guts of those going ashore, and I was thankful that I didn't have to do so myself. After thirty-six hours I was allowed to go off duty, and I slept heavily.

I soon discovered that there was a considerable snag to my new job; the man in charge of our operation was an elderly, retired Royal Navy commander, and his second-in-command was a Frenchman who had somehow found his way into the British Navy. The older man was a bully and the younger sadistic; I was frightened of them both, and whatever skills I had by then developed fled. We had a rota each night, to be officer of the watch, and one night a rating woke me up with an unfavourable weather forecast. I read it and didn't know what to do. I was so nervous of my superior that I did nothing. What I should have done was to pass this information on to the Frenchman. The next morning there was an inquest. To my shame I denied having seen the report, and I repeated this to the rating when he indignantly came to me saying that I had not taken it in. I felt his contempt much deserved, and never stopped feeling guilty about my lack of OLQ (officer-like qualities).

After a few days at moorings the weather worsened and we found shelter in an artificial harbour. This was constructed from old vessels which had been deliberately sunk offshore in order to provide shelter and temporary harbour. The storm blew for several days and there were severe worries about the fate of the expedition because troops and supplies could not be landed. However, eventually things improved. The storm blew itself out and the unpleasant commanding officer and his French mate departed.

The new CO was Lieutenant Commander T. C. S. (Terence Charles Stewart) Morrison Scott. He was an extremely civilised and likeable man, and he treated me and others with affection. He introduced us to such culinary unknowns as Camembert cheese, and also to intelligent conversation. Our workload lessened and eventually became virtually non-existent.

I'd first gone ashore on the third day of the invasion, and we went again to visit the village of Courseulles. There was the smell of battle everywhere, and many damaged buildings, but, as we drove along, the road was lined with residents who cheered us as we passed. We were another group of young men who had not much to do; each morning we fell into the way of sitting round a table, drinking liberal amounts of gin, and again, inevitably, talking amongst other things about sex. By this time in July the sun shone and the weather was hot. The ratings took their matelot shirts off and sunned themselves on deck. It was then, aged nearly twenty-two, that I first admitted to myself that I was physically attracted to my own sex.

I was not particularly upset by this revelation, because I must really have known since I was a young boy. However, this insight did not in any way suggest to me that I might act upon it.

CHAPTER 9

In August we were ordered home. Terence took me on one side and gave me my confidential report – this was positive, saying that I was a good officer and that when I'd overcome my lack of self-confidence I would be a better one.

We reached Southampton and I was sent on indefinite leave. Quite soon I was reunited with Rod, who had also returned from the invasion force, and he stayed with us in Mill Hill. I stayed on leave for two or three months and was then posted to a unit in Dover. The base was a private house on the seafront, and Lieutenant Commander G. was in charge. He had been passed over for promotion in the regular navy, but the war had brought him new responsibilities. He was an amiable man with little self-confidence, and he was an alcoholic. We were based in headquarters attached to the landing craft moored in Dover Harbour, whose crews ferried supplies to the French coast. My duties were not rigorous, and I spent most mornings recording meticulously the numbers of drinks and the takings of the previous evening.

In Dover I made new friends, including Laurie Hinde, Bill Whitehouse-Vaux and Ralph Elliot Laurie – a sweet, amusing man; I seem to have partly denied my earlier sexual insights, because I confided in Laurie that I was thinking of inviting a blonde Wren to stay with me in a hotel in London. He told me that another officer, Freddie, a rather coarse Scotsman, had had a sexual fling with her that had not been successful, and he strongly advised against it. I gratefully accepted his advice. Bill Whitehouse-Vaux was a strange man, but he made a beeline for me and I was flattered by his attention. Bill and I used to go to the same drinking club. Later he married a sweet girl called Joan, and I was best man at the wedding, and later a godfather.

Ralph was keen to be my friend. He took me for a ride in his second-hand car, which kept breaking down, and he invited me to stay with him at his aunt's house, which was nearby. One evening in the unit bathroom, I was standing with my shirt off and Ralph came in and kissed me emphatically on the shoulder. I shouted at him as he retreated through the door.

"It was a joke," he protested.

"It didn't seem like that to me," I said angrily. At that time I had not even begun to deal with my homosexual anxiety.

It was a hot and sunny summer, and in the mornings I used to bathe before breakfast with our petty officer. In the afternoons I sunbathed on the Dover cliffs before going back to the base for tea and early drinks. One day I saw myself in a pub mirror, bronzed and good-looking, and a friend was moved to say that I looked better "now that I had got rid of the shine on my face". In the evenings we piled into a car, driven by the already semi-inebriated Commander G., and headed for the local pubs.

CHAPTER 10

Christmas came and went, and we 'hostility only' ratings waited to be demobilised. Japan had surrendered and it was clear that the navy would soon no longer need us. In March 1946 I went back to Mill Hill with my savings (about £100) and my uniform. I was given a demob suit together with shoes and, I suppose, an overcoat. The suit was perfectly acceptable, but I was too snobbish to wear it. I sold it and bought instead a new suit (which I never liked).

At this stage I made another big life mistake. As a demobilised person I was entitled to go to university with, I think, a two-year limit on deciding to enter. There was a snag because I only had three School Certificate passes and needed five to qualify for university entrance. My friend Frank Jenner, similarly demobilised and unqualified, decided to study for matriculation in order to become a vet. I admired him and knew that matriculating was the sensible thing to do, but my head was full of unrealistic schemes about becoming a playwright and film scriptwriter, which seemed also, quite wrongly, to be an easier option. There was no tradition of university-going in my family, although Vera boasted of her 'Oxford prelims'. Harry fell in with my plan of working in the film business and set about trying to find a contact. While this was going on I began to see a good deal of Bill and Joan Whitehouse-Vaux, and I was best man at their wedding. Bill had decided to use his further-education-and-training grant to enrol in a three-month business-training course, and he urged me to do the same. I foolishly agreed, and this meant that I wasted my grant, which would have got me into university.

On the first morning there was some problem with an officious porter about which entrance to use. I adopted my superior naval-officer tone, but I was quickly brought down to earth by this man; he told me I was nobody in particular now, and that this behaviour cut no ice with him.

As 1946 rolled on, I stayed at home with little money and lowering morale. Vera and I used to go out to lunch (which she paid for). I was given the Den as my room, and I was provided with an old typewriter which had belonged to the bank. On it I wrote a variety of things, though I can't remember what. One piece I do recall, however, was a somewhat blasphemous affair about Jesus. I left it incomplete on the typewriter while I went out. When I got back it had gone. I asked Vera what had happened and she told me that she had thought it unsuitable and had thrown it away. Why didn't I make more of a fuss?

When some petrol became available again, Vera and Harry decided to buy a car. The original plan was for Harry to drive, and, because he had only one arm, we chose a specially adapted second-hand car with automatic gears. This must have been in the days before the driving test – in any event he decided against becoming a driver and left it to Vera. In later years and with later cars her driving and sense of direction were the cause of many rows between them.

Although at first we hired a garage, Harry decided that the Den should be converted into our own garage, and he got planning permission to do this. With the Den gone, I reverted to sleeping in the spare bedroom; this was in no sense mine, and I was liable to be moved out if we had visitors. The furniture consisted of a large double bed, a dressing table and a wardrobe full of Vera's clothes – these smelt musty and had a stale scent. The Den had never been truly mine either, however. Harry and Vera had refused my suggestion that I should entertain my own friends in there, saying that they could be invited into the lounge, where of course they would both be. At least I'd had a measure of privacy, but in the spare room I had little. This was illustrated one evening when I invited a young ex-naval officer whom I'd known in Dover to the house. My parents immediately latched on to him, although in due course we went to 'my' room. Once in there he declared dramatically, "I'm feeling very Oscar Wilde-ish tonight," but a combination of fear of discovery and my own inhibition led to me doing nothing more sinful than going for a walk with him in the park.

The year wore on and I began to be the butt of questions about my future. One particularly humiliating question came from the manageress of the United Dairies, who asked when I was going to get a job. There was a severe winter and a coal shortage, and Vera, Jill and I used to go to the coal depot and load the car with lumps of coal.

Early in 1947 I made contact with Robert McDermott, the script editor of J. Arthur Rank, who was married to a playwright called Diana Morgan.

1947 was a chaotic year for me. I cannot remember how the meeting between Robert McDermott and myself was arranged, but it must have been through a bank contact of Harry's. When I was ushered into his enormous office he was extremely friendly. I think that at this first meeting he gave me a copy of a film adaptation of Hugh Walpole's *Mr Perrin and Mr Traill*, by L. A. G. Strong, then a well-known novelist.

The script seemed to me pedestrian and I tried to lighten it up a little. Some time later the film was shown in the West End; there was no screen credit for me, nor could I detect any of my precious dialogue in the finished article. However, Robert seemed satisfied and told me that I had 'it' (the ability to write), and that he would arrange for me to have a six-month contract with J. Arthur Rank.

After leaving him I went into the West End with a feeling of delight, and I bought my grandmother some rather unsuitable stationery as a present. Some time later I got a contract offering me £15 per week, to be reviewed after six months, with various increasing options. This was unheard-of wealth, and I quickly accepted it and ordered some new and expensive clothes. My delight did not last, but at first all was well because I was sent a selection of other people's stories and scripts and asked to comment on their suitability or otherwise to be turned into films. I was quite good at this, and soon I was asked to adapt scripts of my own.

Although I didn't realise it the Rank empire was beginning to totter; some expensive films had not made money, and change was in the air. I was assigned to Highbury Studios as a trainee scriptwriter. The man in charge of production was John Croydon, a remote and, to me, forbidding figure. He had been hired to produce a series of fairly short and cheap second features to be programmed with the main film. He handed me a novel called *Brensham Village* and asked me to adapt it. *Brensham Village* had no consistent storyline, as I recall it now, but was a series of vignettes of village life. I found it extremely difficult to produce any coherent script, and each time I went to see him with my latest attempt, he kept me waiting – sometimes for several hours. When I was eventually called in, he would sit behind his desk and read everything I had written, whilst saying nothing. He must have talked to me, but I can only remember being certain that he did not like my work, and that each revision was no improvement.

One morning I woke up and decided that I could not go on. When my mother came into the bedroom I simply said, "I can't cope." I spent several days in bed and felt enormous relief. I told Harry and Vera that I did not want to go on, and that I had made up my mind to cancel my contract. They were much against this, and they persuaded me to write to John Croydon saying that I had flu and would contact him when I had recovered.

The family doctor visited and I steeled myself to tell him of my increasing anxieties about my sexuality. He quickly made it clear that he didn't want to hear anything about this, and he told my parents that what I needed was a cruise 'on a banana boat' – and so it was arranged. At considerable expense they booked me on to a ship called the *Alca*, and I travelled to Liverpool to board her. I knew that the right plan would have been for me not to go on board but to get the next train back to London. However, my passivity as usual took over and I joined the good ship *Alca*.

The *Alca* had two functions: it ferried tomatoes and bananas from the Canary Islands, and it also acted as a cruise ship for mainly middle-class, middle-income passengers. The whole trip of ten days was something of a jumbled nightmare. I shared a cabin with an elderly man who had religious mania. Thankfully he disembarked after a few days and I was then on my own. Other passengers tried to befriend me, but I was locked into my own miseries and found it hard to respond. Although I had learned to drink in the navy, I don't recall drinking much while on board. The food seemed extraordinary considering the privations of austere Britain, and we pursued our way through many courses.

One day I felt so miserable that I did not get up. I'd become friendly with a nice general practitioner and his wife, and he took the trouble to visit me in my cabin. They had obviously already realised that I was in emotional trouble, and he actually tried to get me to talk. "Sometimes young people do have sexual worries and I wonder if these are troubling you?" he said. I shook my head and rebuffed his well-intentioned question. What a pity!

I wrote a long and careful letter to Vera and Harry, explaining that I was unsuited to the film business and intended to resign, but again passivity took over and I did not send it. I have little recollection of the Canary Islands, or even of where we visited. An older man tried to take me under his wing, but I found him uninteresting, although he was kind to me.

On the last night the passengers and crew were supposed to put on a review: 'The Alca Revellers'. I can only remember reluctantly joining a line of dancing couples and thinking that this nightmare was nearly over. On the next morning we said our goodbyes on the jetty. One lady passenger of a certain age, who had been having an affair with one of the ships officers, sat disconsolately on her suitcase, her sexual dream/adventure over, at least for the time being.

The nice general practitioner and his wife received a telegram saying that their daughter had developed poliomyelitis. He burst into tears. The right-wing, middle-class couple and I got into the same train compartment, but she explained that it would be best if we travelled separately. I think that by then I was regarded as odd – also, at the bar I had ventured some radical opinions.

Harry and Vera met me at the Mill Hill bus stop. I suppose that I was tanned, and they must have hoped that my 'nervous breakdown' had been cured. Unfortunately it had not been, and I told them straight away that I was still not feeling properly well. The disappointment on their faces was obvious, and I was sorry for them. We went home and were soon discussing my future. I was adamant that I wanted to resign, but I was persuaded that I must go back to John Croydon.

I made the journey to Highbury with considerable anxiety. As usual there was a long wait; the secretary began talking to me and said that she thought that people only became writers because they couldn't help themselves. I was edgy and paranoid and took this as some sort of dig at me, although I don't suppose that it was. Eventually John Croydon summoned me and told me that my contract wouldn't be renewed. He added that it would be possible to end it early if I so wished. I had no idea what, if anything, I replied.

Winter was approaching, and as I travelled home on the bus rain streamed down the windows. I felt lost, humiliated, and I wished that I'd followed my instincts and simply resigned. Harry and Vera were indignant, and Harry told me that on no account was I to forfeit any money due to me.

CHAPTER 11

I had no idea what to do next. Somehow I filled in my time, sometimes by going to the cinema. One day I went to a showing of Leni Riefenstahl's *Olympia* at the old Scala cinema near Tottenham Court Road, and I deliberately chose to sit next to a young man whom I had seen in there once before.

Quite soon he moved his knee next to mine, and we remained in this position for most of the film. When the lights went up he smiled and we left together. He invited me to have tea with him at a nearby café, and he told me that his name was Kieran Tunney and that he was a playwright. I was much impressed, and when we parted he asked for my phone number. I went home feeling rather more cheerful, and I was flattered when he telephoned soon afterwards. "Somebody with such a nice voice wants to speak to you," said Vera, and indeed he did have a gentle voice, with a slight Irish accent.

Kieran invited me to go to the theatre with him to see *Red Roses for Me*. This invitation raised my extremely low self-esteem and I eagerly awaited our meeting. In some sense I must have known what I was letting myself in for, but I chose not to think about the possible consequences. After the theatre Kieran took me out to supper and then invited me back to his room in Mayfair. Over a drink he told me that he wrote, together with a friend. What really fascinated me, however, was that he had recently come back from a meeting with Tallulah Bankhead in the USA. He told me that he'd written a play and was hoping that she would star in it, although he thought her a little old for the part.

All this was caviar conversation to me, and no doubt my subconscious was working overtime, as when I looked at my watch it was too late for the Underground. We walked to Marble Arch in the vain hope that there might be a bus. In the end there seemed nothing for it but to accept Kieran's offer to go back to his room. I telephoned home, telling them that I'd been invited to a party and would be back in the morning. Kieran had a double bed, and I self-consciously stripped down to my unfashionable 'winter woollen' pants before climbing in gingerly beside him. After a pause he flung one arm round me, from which I recoiled. "Who do you think that I am, Ann Todd?" I said, somewhat dramatically. Kieran withdrew, and I suppose he realised that he'd taken on board a mixed-up boy. He explained that he could make love to either sex, and he seemed genuinely taken aback. I told him that I would sleep on the floor, but he refused this and said that he'd stay with his uncle, who lived nearby. In the end we both remained in the bed, and when he was asleep I had a fierce desire to explore his body. In the morning we made awkward farewells. He told me rather bitchily that I wasn't really his type nor his intellectual equal. Looking back I now feel sorry for him; he wasn't to know that I was emotionally disturbed, nor did I understand that I was behaving like an insufferable little prick-teaser!

By the time I got home I knew that something quite fundamental was going on inside me. I felt acutely anxious and guilty and that there was nobody with whom I could discuss what I'd done (or, in reality, not done). I cannot remember at all what I did during the next few days. The tension became unbearable and I decided that I'd have to tell my father. This was in contrast to my earlier episode with Coombe, when I told my mother and excluded Harry. I asked him if he would go to the cinema with me, and we saw a film called *Quiet Wedding*. I sat through this comedy wondering if I was going to begin our discussion; but, when I actually did, Harry was extremely supportive. I told him about Kieran and of my quite unrealistic fear that he would be broadcasting our encounter. Harry accepted my concern at face value, and said that we'd take action if this should happen. I told him that I was "afraid that I was going the other way".

Somehow we got on to his own experiences in the Great War. "I wasn't a saint," he told me. I assumed he was talking of heterosexual experiences, although years later my analyst speculated that these might have been homosexual. We agreed that Vera wouldn't be told of our discussion.

Harry must have thought that my confiding in him would set me right, and indeed in the beginning it did. I felt tremendous relief, as if a terrible weight had lifted, but soon a new demon appeared. I became anxious that, by confiding in him, I might cause him untold and unspecified damage, although I couldn't tell him this. I think it must have been at this point that he again produced the nice bank doctor: he referred me to an eminent psychiatrist in Harley Street.

This man looked like an elderly bird. I blurted out my worries about homosexuality. His voice was crisp and dry, and it was clear that he thought I was getting things out of proportion. He asked me about my mother, and when I described her as a vivacious woman who should have been an actress he nodded. I guessed that she was appearing to him, quite correctly, as the powerful mother of this distressed and passive son. He asked what homosexual experience I'd had, and when I replied none (give or take Coombe) he suggested heartily that I should try some. He ended by saying that he didn't think that I was homosexual, and that I should get out and about and make new friends of both sexes. This was perfectly sensible advice, but it didn't in any way speak to my condition.

I continued to deteriorate. The next thing that happened was that I began to feel empty and shut off from other people. I'd entered the black world of the severely depressed. Although I'd been depressed as a boy it had been readily cured by a holiday in Margate with Harry, so this was my first experience of the netherworld. It's a curious place to be, unlike any other that I've known. The mornings were the worst: I woke suddenly and early and in despair. It seemed all too clear that this was to be my normal state from now on, and that my former ability to enjoy the world had been an illusion. This was reality. I had no wish to get out of bed and no inclination to do anything. Vera knew something of my state, and she said, correctly, that depression was much worse than a physical illness or a broken limb. One morning I got into her empty bed, pulled the sheets over my head and tried, in a half-hearted and histrionic way, to suffocate.

My parents did their best. I went to see the local vicar, a worldly young man who suggested that I become a visitor to a local boy who had congenital syphilis. I went once and have no idea what we talked about; I never went back. He also suggested that I repair some of the church's battered hymn books, and I found this therapeutic. Vera had a friend who was a masseur and who had marital troubles. She massaged my feet with powder and we each silently communicated to the other our respective grief.

As each day wore on, I noticed that I felt less awful in the late afternoons, and that this seemed to coincide with Harry's return from work. By bedtime I could think that perhaps it would all go away. Early the next morning, however, it was clear that there was to be no escape.

Marjorie, our next-door neighbour, was consulted. She suggested that I go to stay at her sister's farm in North Wales, where Peter and I had stayed as children. I agreed to go, despite knowing that nothing anyone could do would make a difference. The household consisted of Marjorie's sister (a dominating woman without Marjorie's eccentricity or charm), her sat-upon husband (Willem), and their two children (Peter and Meryl). The children led rather isolated lives and welcomed me, odd though I was. Marjorie's sister said that she couldn't remember my name and made up a different one, by which she called me throughout my visit.

The days had their own routine. Peter called me early, although I was generally already awake. We had breakfast and then got to work on the farm. While it was still dark, my first duty was to slop out the pigs, and later on we did hedging and ditching. In the afternoons I was 'lent' to a friend of Peter's who was a gardener. He was a pleasant, young married man, about whom Peter hinted darkly that, "He likes his own sex too much." Peter ran the farm and his father was very much second in command. When the day's work was finished we all ate together, then Willem went to the pub and we three young ones made our own entertainment. Meryl had the records of *Oklahoma*, and we played these over and over. One evening we went to the cinema and saw a Hollywood musical, and this seemed quite an event.

I found that, as at home, the mornings were simply a time to be endured, but that by the evening I could be some company for Peter and Meryl. I was still preoccupied by my fear that I'd damaged Harry in some way and that this might prove fatal. After perhaps a fortnight I went home. As before, I had to face Vera and Harry's disappointment that I was no better. Looking back I can only admire the tenacious efforts they made to get their son back.

They finally managed this, thanks to a long-standing friend of Harry's called Uncle Monty. He was a rather mysterious and glamorous figure to me. In earlier days he and Harry had gone on walking holidays, from which Vera and Monty's wife, Nell, were excluded. He was a doctor, and we had seen a good deal of him before the war. For unexplained reasons he'd temporarily retired, and he and Nell had taken a flat near us. Monty and Nell were telephoned, and quite soon I was on the train to Bristol, taking my rations with me. They made me welcome, and it soon became clear that they had both suffered from 'nerves' and sympathised with my condition. Over the next few months I made several visits, during the first of which I told Monty of my shameful secret. He was not at all shocked, and during the next few months he and I became extremely close. He had private rooms in Bristol, and he asked a physician colleague to examine me. He then X-rayed my pelvis, on the grounds that there was a theory that male homosexuals had wider hips than heterosexuals. Another procedure involved testing urine to establish whether the hormonal levels differed.

I visited one weekend while Nell was away, and the real reason for my X-ray became apparent. It was a sunny day, and Monty and I went to a neighbour's drinks party. When we came back pleasantly drunk, we changed into shorts and sunbathed on the flat roof. Monty then told me that he was a hypocrite – he'd been plagued all his life by his own homosexuality, but had not felt able to tell me this until now. This information really completed my recovery, but it also produced a new problem: it was obvious that Monty was physically attracted to me, but I didn't return his feelings. I thought he was old – he must have been in his early fifties. Although he made his attraction known, he didn't pursue it. Looking back it would have been kinder if I'd offered him some comfort, but I was too scared and ruthless to do this. I think that Nell must have been suspicious, and perhaps jealous of our relationship. Monty liked alcohol, as I did, and Nell used to go to bed early, leaving him and me to talk freely, often about sexual matters. She would complain about the "gales of laughter" she could hear in the sitting room, from which she felt excluded.

One story Monty told me was of an encounter with Beverley Nichols in Paris. Beverley Nichols was then a well-known writer, and he tended to give advice on religious matters. Monty and he had sex together, and all would have been well had he not then written about how he had 'saved this unhappy doctor'. The story got into the Bristol press, to Monty's great embarrassment, although he was not named. I believe that this episode led to, or was part of the reason for, his retiring temporarily to London.

Nell had a tragic family history. Her mother was still alive, the wife of a Methodist minister, and she had three brothers – one a missionary and another a clergyman. The third had also been a clergyman and had died in a violent way. He was depressive and drank a great deal. He was also, I gathered from Monty, homosexual. Eventually, he had cut his throat and Monty was summoned. He spoke proudly of having cleared up all the blood and restoring some sort of order in the vicarage.

Nell was also a depressive, and she had had a severe episode after the cot death of their baby son. Monty's reaction had been to feel guilty that he'd been responsible, in some unexplained way, because of his sexuality. They had an older daughter, Pat, whom in earlier days I'd been thought a suitable partner for. However, she had chosen Gordon and had gone to live in Kenya. It was my contact with Nell and Monty which brought me back to normality, and I continued to see them, although less often as my life moved on.

CHAPTER 12

I still had no clear idea of what to do, although because of Monty's friendship I began to consider the idea of studying medicine. I was twenty-five, had no money and a large lack of skills in physics and chemistry, both necessary in order to pass first MB. This was in fact quite a crazy idea, and it illustrates not only my own feelings of omnipotence, but also a continuing lack of knowledge of who I really was as a person.

In the meantime I had to earn my living. I had kept in touch with a man on the business training course, and over a drink he told me there was a vacancy in the Space Buying Department at Everetts' advertising agency in Mayfair. I went for an interview and was appointed as Space Buyer's Assistant for £6 a week.

Before joining the department I spent some time in other departments, including Media Planning. This was run by a powerful forty-year-old called Mary Davie, and her younger assistant, Joan. What I didn't realise was that Space Buying and Media Planning were two rival organisations. The Space Buyer was Miss Higgs, uncertain of her social class and alcoholic. Mary Davie by contrast had the arrogant certainty of the upper middle class. Miss Higgs operated mainly by instinct, while Mary relied on figures and statistics. The Hulton survey, then fashionable, was a shared joke in Media Planning: its tables 'were broken down by age and sex'.

While I was attached to Media Planning, Mary asked me to write an essay (though I can't remember what about). She showed me one written by a previous trainee, and she said how good it was. Although I was much better, I was still deeply anxious and unsure of myself and kept a bottle of valerian, supplied by Vera, in my raincoat pocket, from which I took occasional swigs. I felt that I couldn't cope with this essay, and so after Mary and Joan had gone I took the earlier essay out of the desk and rewrote this over the weekend, disguising it as best I could and passing it off as my own work. On Monday morning I put it back in the drawer and, when Mary arrived, gave her my own version. She read it through and then said, "It's quite like Tony's; it's almost as if . . . But no, it can't possibly be . . ." I think that she didn't seriously suspect, and for once I didn't feel guilty.

Eventually I had to join Miss Higgs, her second in command (Mr Chrisford, known as Chris), and two girls (Mary and Doris). I hated this job, feeling quite accurately that Space Buying was below the salt compared with other departments. However, I had to make the best of a complicated situation. Miss Higgs ran a tight ship when she was sober; she arrived in the morning carefully and freshly dressed and made us work hard until about noon. After noon, though, the newspapers' space-sellers often took her out for long lunches from which she might not come back until mid-afternoon. By then she would be loquacious and often aggressive, and her dress not quite so immaculate. Her return could be heard throughout the building, and there were stories that when drunk she was given to making passes in the ladies' lavatory. What I had not realised was that Miss Higgs' alcoholism was 'a best kept secret that everybody knew', and I suspected that I'd been brought in to restore some stability to the department.

Another cause of my unhappiness was that I didn't get on with Mary and Doris. As soon as Miss Higgs departed, they chatted and gossiped and made it difficult to work. I think that because of my ambivalence towards women, I behaved stupidly, being extremely critical and asking them to get on with their work. Eventually they complained to Miss Higgs about my attitude.

With my self-confidence somewhat restored, I asked to see Mr Linford, one of the directors. He was an extremely nice man and clearly understood the problems. Within days he had offered me and Chris new jobs as assistant Space Buyers and I had a fifty per cent pay rise – up to £9 a week.

I became friendly both with Mary Davie and Joan. Rumour was that Mary had been married three times and she had one son called Julian. We often went to lunch together, and this meant that I might be a few minutes late in getting back. If Miss Higgs were at her desk she'd look at her watch in silent disapproval.

Mary was studying at the London School of Economics for an economics degree. She told me that, when she got her degree, "I should be looking for at least a thousand a year." With her powerful intelligence I foresaw no problem with this, but I was wrong. After sitting the examination, she told me that either they would think her papers were brilliant, although unorthodox, or she would fail. When the results arrived she telephoned, saying, "Michael, the news is bad, very bad." Mary left Everetts and got a job with the John Lewis Partnership. She joked that the staff were careful with the pencils because they all owned them. I think she was deeply disappointed, although she hid this.

I continued to see her until she died in the early 1960s. By then she had heart disease and had also become a rather unlikely Quaker. One of the last things I remember her telling me was that she was having a dispute over noise with a restaurant near her house. I asked what she was going to do. "I'm going to try the Quaker way first," she replied.

I had a different relationship with Joan, who was then living with Michael Ayrton, the artist. The relationship was troubled, and Michael was having an affair. Joan was pretty and articulate, but she lacked assurance and had a poor self-image. We made a good pair. One evening we had a drink and then went back to her and Michael's flat for supper. Soon after we got there she complained that it was hot and stepped neatly out of her knickers. I didn't know how to respond, and I pretended that I'd not noticed. Joan must have realised that I was going to be unsuitable material as a lover, but it didn't prevent us from becoming good friends. Once, however, to my chagrin, she responded to something I was telling her by saying, "But my dear girl–" before she stopped herself. She was knowledgeable about the arts and knew Margot Fonteyn and Constant Lambert.

CHAPTER 13

I had developing ambitions to become a medical student, so I enrolled in the matriculation department of the Regent Street Polytechnic. Joan and I finished work at 5.50 p.m. and we then walked to Oxford Circus, where I went into the poly and she into her flat near Broadcasting House. I studied French and English literature, physics, chemistry and maths. Although I'd never been able to learn at school, this now seemed possible. Each evening lasted from 6 p.m. till 9 p.m., and of course there was also homework to be done. By now I'd found a small flat in Swiss Cottage, which was another attempt at independence.

As if I were not busy enough, Bill Whitehouse-Vaux persuaded me to play rugby for the RNVR team on Saturday afternoons. Also I used to run round the block before breakfast and then quite often cycled from the flat in Swiss Cottage to Mayfair. I can't understand why I agreed to play rugby, especially as I played extremely badly. At school I'd gone to great lengths to avoid this unpleasant game, and I now dreaded getting the white card telling me where I would play next. I think it must have been masochistic, but I also believe it somehow made me feel better about myself. The best part for me was the communal bath afterwards, when we young men all bathed together in a homoerotic ritual. The main point of my life at that time was to fill up every minute, except Sundays when I went home, so that at the end of the day I could say to myself, "Now I can take the screws off."

I stayed at the Regent Street Polytechnic for two years, 1948–9, and was then faced with taking the London matriculation exam. Although I knew that in first MB I would have to pass in physics and chemistry, unreality took over and I took only the arts subjects and maths. I passed in these and was now, at the age of twenty-seven, at last ready to go to university. I wrote to all the London medical schools and got an interview at the London Hospital in Whitechapel. They asked me why I wanted to be a doctor, to which I replied, "I want to help." It's debatable whom I wanted to help, but I'm pretty sure that it was myself rather than anybody else.

I next had to finance myself. I applied for a major county award and got one worth £180 a year. Long-suffering Harry gave me £10 a month, and a letter to the *News of the World*, which in those days ran a column for deserving causes, brought £50. Much to my surprise, the managing director of Everetts called me in, wished me luck and gave me £50. I left Everetts in quite a blaze of glory, only slightly diminished by Miss Higgs, who said, "I don't see this boy making a doctor."

In the summer of 1950 I went to a work camp in the south of France. This was a project to restore a village for destitute children. It was extremely hot and we were digging a stream known as 'La Source'. I travelled with a London Hospital student who had already taken first MB and he told me about the lectures and what I'd be in for. I became extremely bronzed and fit, and I spent a few days on the way back in a tented village in Paris, with a young man called Peter whom I met at the camp. He had lost a leg in the war, but he was extremely competent and laughed at my nervousness in finding my way around the city.

I had by then given up my flat and gone home to Mill Hill. Back at home I felt full of energy and optimism about my new beginning. I was keen to tell Vera of my adventures, but she wearied of these because she wanted to tell me about her own life while I'd been away.

CHAPTER 14

I had to study for first MB at Queen Mary College, in Mile End Road. On the appointed morning, I set off feeling very much that it was like my first day at a new school. When I arrived there was much socialising and jockeying for suitable new friends. As an ex-naval officer, who had subsequently also worked in the film business, I was seen as something of a catch. I felt a fraud on both counts, although I was pleased to be able to bring this reputation with me. The student intake consisted of a few 'veterans' like me, some more who had done national service, and the majority who had just left school. Shy as I was, I had the pick of the student year to choose as friends. On the whole, passive as ever, I waited for them to come to me. The two nearest to me were Tony Hicklin and John, whom I preferred and who was another mirror of my own low self-esteem.

After a day or two we started serious studying and I began to realise what I'd taken on. I'd never been any good at either physics or chemistry (Mr Stanley at school had certainly not helped). I was aware that many of those around me were strong in science subjects, while I only felt comfortable with the arts. I worked hard and wrote up my notes conscientiously, but within weeks my brittle self-confidence collapsed and I decided that this was to be yet another failure in my life. I cannot remember whom I told, but it appeared that I was not going to be allowed to collapse yet again; out of the blue (or so it seemed) a friendly demonstrator made himself known and offered to give me free extra tuition in these impossible subjects. As a result I passed in chemistry, botany and zoology, but was referred in physics. This result was better than I'd expected, although it meant I would have to study for an extra term while my successful colleagues moved along the Whitechapel Road to the hospital to begin studying for second MB. On the other hand there was a considerable winnowing at this stage, and many students gave up medicine altogether.

During this year I'd made two more particular friends: one was Joe Connolly, whom I greatly admired, and the other was Alan Bussey. Alan at first admired me because of my background, but when he had to relate to the real person I was not to his liking. He had an American friend, I. D., who was fairly overtly homosexual and who gave up after a year; but Alan also picked this up from me, and this together with my academic performance made him fairly contemptuous of me.

I took a holiday job and went back to Queen Mary College for another term in autumn 1951. I was able to concentrate entirely on physics, and the department seemed determined to get me through, although it must have been rather like teaching a monkey to type the Lord's Prayer. When it came to the practical, I had to do two experiments, one on light and the other setting up an electrical circuit. Dr Irons, who was in charge of the department, was on hand and he inspected my work. When it came to the electrical circuit even he seemed to find difficulty. He said, "Barker [his assistant] set this up." Everyone, especially me, was relieved when I passed and moved up the road to the hospital.

By now my former colleagues were settled in, whilst I had to face a new set of challenges. John and I clung together in this difficult world. He was a dental student and he had a different curriculum, but we played squash and went on a week's canoeing holiday, sharing a tent. I was of course physically attracted to him, and our physical closeness made me embarrassed. However, sex wasn't discussed between us.

The worst part of my new studies was the anatomy vivas. Each group of students was assigned a dead and pickled body, and we had to dissect it in various parts. At first we were shocked, but quite soon we became blasé about this bizarre activity. When the group felt confident (I never did) about their dissection they asked an anatomy demonstrator for a viva. These were pleasant and tolerant young men who were, I suppose, training to climb the academic ladder. We also had lectures and I remember most clearly one in which the anatomy professor told us with slides about the first sex change operation from man to woman.

I found physiology relatively easy, but pharmacology rather passed me by. I spent the next five terms studying hard and foolishly avoiding most of the clubs and activities which my peers enjoyed. I did keep up with Joe Connolly, however, who still seemed to admire me in spite of my shortcomings. I was referred again, this time in anatomy, and spent another term revising this subject. Again the powers that be seemed determined to get me through, and at the practical exam I was taken round by a friendly demonstrator who smilingly muttered "nominal aphasia" when I could not remember the name of an artery or nerve. The anatomy department was on the first floor, and when I discovered that I'd passed I was met at the foot of the stairs by Joe, by now the editor of the hospital gazette. He asked me if I'd join him as co-editor, and I was so elated and flattered that I agreed.

In the meantime there had been changes at Mill Hill. Harry had had a threatened heart attack and decided to retire early. He'd been appointed staff controller of the bank, and this may have been one step too far. He and Vera put the house on the market and eventually sold it to my sister Jill and her recent husband, Ken. I went with the house. Vera and Harry set off on a long driving tour of England before eventually buying a cottage in a Devon village. They stayed there for a while, then made a highly unsuccessful move to Oxford and eventually settled in Sidmouth.

Passing second MB was by no means the end of my difficulties. We were allotted to firms, and my first assignment was for a three-month stint with a surgical firm run by a tough consultant called Hermon Taylor. His teaching was not much fun for the patients, and none at all for people like me who hid at the back of the group and couldn't give the correct answer even if they knew it.

In addition to this I promised Joe my help on the gazette. He provided a typewriter and we sat together one evening working on the next edition. My brain refused to function and I found myself unable to type words correctly. I didn't know what to do and consulted Ken, who had a clear brain. He told me correctly that I'd feel guilty if I gave up the job, but overwhelmed if I continued to try to do it. I went to see Joe, and over a drink I told him that I couldn't carry on. He was angry and disappointed and said, "Michael, have you ever needed responsibility as much as you do now?" He found another co-editor – a job which would have incidently almost guaranteed me a house job at the London.

All this led me not only to feel guilty, but also to try to cope with my duties at the surgical firm. I became increasingly phobic about the ward rounds, and I eventually went to see the dean, Harry May. Harry wasn't a clinician, but he dealt with this sympathetically and, as he saw it, rationally. He accepted my view that I was unsuited to being a medical student and that I should resign. It was unclear at thirty-one what I could do next, but I felt great relief and went round all my patients writing up their notes; then I went home with my responsibilities abandoned.

I remember going to see a film one afternoon called *How to Marry a Millionaire*, which I managed to enjoy, but I realised that I was running away from real life. One day the phone rang; it was a student friend, Helen Linn, a former nurse and also someone who didn't find studying easy. She asked me what on earth I thought I was doing, and that a number of student colleagues were worried about me. They had been to see the new dean, John Ellis, and she suggested that I did so too. I agreed. John Ellis was a very different man from Harry May; he was a clinician, a medical consultant, and he was interested in emotional things. He quickly picked up how disturbed I was, and he asked if I would see his psychiatrist colleague, Pat Tooley. I agreed, and I remember getting my hair cut very short for my appointment (why on earth, I wonder?).

Pat was a benign, charming man, and I soon told him of my troubles: not only was I a homosexual, but I couldn't possibly cope with the clinical school curriculum. He seemed unconcerned about my sexuality and asked if he could get my scholastic record. I suspect he thought that I was a perfectionist who was really doing reasonably well. When I saw him again he didn't refer to this, and I realised that I'd given him an accurate picture of my floundering career. He was, however, positive and encouraging, and he managed to massage me back into university life.

I went back reluctantly and resentfully. I thanked Helen for her intervention and took her to see Beatrice Lilley in a show. After it she said, "You didn't seem to enjoy that very much." In truth I was again depressed, and I saw no way out of my troubles. I decided to go back to Hermon Taylor's surgical firm.

I felt duty-bound to go back to the place I'd deserted, but Hermon Taylor was still intimidating. He told me that the ward rounds were just 'good fun' and he asked if I'd ever broken down before, but at least he left me alone at the back of the group.

Jill and Ken had to share my misery, and Ken, who'd had some contact with a Jungian therapist, suggested I go to see him as well. I poured out my troubles, to which he finally responded by saying, "I think you are in hell." He advised me to give up medicine and also suggested putting my name forward to the Jungian group, the Society for Analytical Psychology, saying they had a special scheme for badly off people like myself.

Sometime later I was invited to see a Mrs Jean Rees, an analyst who lived in West Hampstead. A few days after I first met her, I dreamed that I had a wound on my forehead and had to visit a prostitute who lived up a flight of stairs and who would cure me. On the day of my appointment I found the right door, climbed the stairs and met Mrs Rees. She was understandably impressed by my dream and interpreted it. She was a friendly, quite forceful woman and we got on well. I told her I was disappointed not to have a male therapist, but she said that it wouldn't matter in the long run.

Later I came to believe that it made more sense for me to see a woman. At the beginning she smoked, as I did, and when she got out a cigarette I leaned forward with a lighter, from which she recoiled. I felt rejected, and later on I told her this. "It was one of my mistakes," she said, although she had by then given up smoking.

I went to see her for sixteen years, sometimes two, three or five times a week, depending on where I was and how urgent my need. It's extremely difficult to recall what happened in these sessions. At first we sat face-to-face, but later she persuaded me to lie on the couch. I associate this with her moving to quite a grand house, in St John's Wood. For the first year I wrote an account of each session after it had happened, which I've not looked at since. When I told her that I'd stopped writing these accounts she seemed relieved, because I suppose she thought I would become more spontaneous.

I told her that the other therapist had advised me to give up medicine. She clearly disagreed with him and said, "But you are going on with it, aren't you?"

I must have been an enormously difficult patient, and, without realising, I used every trick I knew to disarm her and, I suppose, keep her off the scent. I fed her lots of information, and because I could be amusing some of our sessions were quite chatty ones. Quite soon I decided that she must be the analyst author Joanna Field (whose real name was Marion Milner), who had written a book that impressed me called *On Not Being Able To Paint*. It took a while for her to tell me that this wasn't so. On a fantasy level I decided that she was my mother and that John was my father, because they seemed to be the two adults who were looking after me (and, although I didn't consciously recognise it, helping me to grow).

Some time into the analysis she changed gear and told me she realised our sessions were too social and enjoyable (I'm sure these were not her words, but the meaning was plain enough). What I didn't understand at the time was that because I was 'on the panel' I had been assigned a student analyst. I guessed that her supervisor had picked up what was going on.

At the hospital, my recollection is that there were two surgical firms and two medical. I can only remember the two medical ones so perhaps I missed one of the surgical firms. I went on to work under John Ellis, which is an indication that he wanted to keep an eye on me. He had a caustic wit, and he assigned me to 'clerk' a highly neurotic woman, saying that she and I had a lot in common. The consultant at the other medical firm was Sir Horace, later Lord Evans, who had an extensive private practice. Often he didn't appear and the round would be taken by his senior registrar; when he did come he was friendly and gracious and never asked the students any questions.

The three patients I remember best are a young woman who had a then rare disease called disseminated lupus erythematosus. I 'clerked' her and she created great medical interest. The second was a young boy with nephritis; his face and body were swollen and it was, I suppose, in the days before dialysis by chemical means. Leeches were tried, with no success, and then fine tubes were inserted into his legs. As the fluid drained away we saw what a shrunken little person he really was. The third patient came later on. I used to go to John Ellis's outpatient clinic, where we were given a patient to interview and examine. Mine was a young man with a number of physical symptoms, but also emotional ones, which I recognised only too readily. John Ellis said, "What is your diagnosis, Doctor?" and I said, "Depression." John Ellis agreed, and he couldn't keep the surprise out of his voice that I'd made what would have been for others a difficult diagnosis.

After the three-monthly firms we formed another smaller group, which was attached to different specialities for a month. These included such subjects as obstetrics; gynaecology; ear, nose and throat; ophthalmology; etc. Psychiatry got a low priority, being shared with skin.

The groups bonded closely and I am still in touch with some of the members. The speciality I remember most clearly was obstetrics. Each student had to deliver twenty babies, and these deliveries were often in the small houses in the Whitechapel area. Our group gathered nervously and waited for our first summons. When it came I was so frightened that I bolted out of the door before anyone else could offer their services. I met an experienced midwife and we made our way to a house nearby. The midwife carried a capacious bag, which she put on the floor, and the woman on the bed groaned in labour. The midwife said, "Doctor will open the bag and get out the rubber sheet." She knew that I was completely ignorant, and also afraid, and while giving me credit for the delivery took charge of it herself. It was an extraordinary feeling when the baby's head appeared, then its body slithered out. The umbilical cord was tied and then cut, and I felt truly that I was in touch with some mysterious and profound process which I'd never experienced before.

Some deliveries took place at the hospital when difficulties were expected; episiotomies were sometimes performed by the students. After the delivery, the cut had to be sewn up again, and sometimes the students also did this. I remember one hearty midwife hoisting the new mother up with her legs apart, turning on the light so we could see what we were doing, and announcing, "Spotlight on charm!"

By now I was more involved with life at the medical school. Joe remained friendly although more distant, and he invited me to write articles for the gazette. I moved into the student hostel and began to feel that I belonged. I declined an offer to help with the script for the Christmas pantomime, but I took a more lowly position as a scene-shifter. I feigned an interest in the rugby team and ran along the touchline shouting, in a faintly ridiculous way, "Up the London!"

The boys and girls with whom I'd started out were by now taking their finals, while I was still in the foothills. One young man said to me patronisingly, "At this rate I shall be a registrar before you even qualify."

But there were casualties; the one that affected me most deeply was John's death, which had taken place some time previously. After I'd recovered from my second breakdown and had gone back to the hospital, John in turn became depressed. He was involved with a girl, and this seemed to be causing him difficulties, although he didn't discuss these with me. He was admitted to the Maudsley Hospital where he was given ECT. I visited him there and after a few treatments he was allowed home for the weekend. He came to see me in Mill Hill and said, "Michael, don't ever let this happen to you."

For some reason I was on my own in the house when the telephone rang early one morning; it was John's father. "Johnnie's done it," he said. The night before he had gone downstairs and put his head in the gas oven. In his belongings they found syringes and other paraphernalia. I took an amphetamine tablet, went to the dental school and told them what had happened. Later I went to his funeral. I know that his parents wanted me to stay in touch, but I felt overwhelmed, and to my regret I never contacted them again.

There were other casualties. The sweet girl Mary developed schizophrenia. She managed to get a house job, but I have no idea what happened to her after that. Peter, who was something of a friend and a clever student, became depressed and had to be admitted to the local psychiatric unit. At least two other students whom I knew broke down in various ways. Being a medical student was a stressful occupation, and the jolly romps portrayed by Dirk Bogarde et al were not the whole story.

While my colleagues were beginning to qualify and get house jobs, either at the London or elsewhere, I was struggling with exams. We were all expected to take the London University degree in medicine and surgery (MBBS), and as an insurance policy many also sat for the membership of the Royal College of Surgeons and also the Royal College of Physicians (MRCS LRCP). The advantage of this second qualification was that it could be taken bit by bit, whereas the university exam had to be passed in one go or with a referral in only one subject. I started on a slow path by sitting for the MRCS LRCP subject by subject. I failed sometimes, but by degrees I passed in all the relevant subjects and became a doctor.

CHAPTER 15

It was 1958. I had mixed feelings about qualifying; on the one hand I felt triumphant that UCS hadn't grasped my potential and thought that I was suitable for clerical work ("Are you mad boy?"), and I basked in congratulations. My grandmother sent me £50. But, on the other hand, I now actually had to do something. I was obviously not going to get a house job at the London, but there was a clearing house for posts available at other hospitals. I applied for a locum job at the Dreadnought Seamen's Hospital in Greenwich and was accepted. I was terrified and read the Houseman's handbook page by page. How could I possibly cope with taking blood, putting up intravenous drips and doing lumbar punctures when I'd never done these before? As usual my fears were worse than the reality. The staff at Greenwich seemed delighted to have me and made no attempt to make me do procedures beyond my ability. There was no emergency surgery, and the surgeon for whom I held 'knives and forks' was considerate – a far cry from the Hermon Taylors of this world.

My confidence was a little restored. Tom Bucher, a friend from our days at the London, had just finished a surgical house job at the Whittington Hospital, and he said I could probably get it. I went for the interview and one of the questions was about my age. When I replied, "Thirty-six," the questioner looked puzzled and said, "Do you mean twenty-six?" At that stage I looked much younger than my real age, and I believed that my outer appearance matched my inner immaturity (indeed, Mrs Rees told me many years later that when I first started my analysis I looked like an old baby).

I was appointed, and I started a six-month job on a surgical unit. The consultant was Neville Stidolph, who was a decent, kindly man. My first three months were spent on the genito-urinary ward. The sister was a real cow, and she lost no opportunity in making me feel small. "Hurry up, hurry up!" she breathed at my side as I tried to get intravenous blood, and at first my appearance with a syringe was greeted by the patients with dismay. Quite suddenly, however, rather like riding a bicycle, I got the knack, as I did eventually with the other procedures I had dreaded so much. I even managed to give intravenous fluids to a baby, which is a difficult manoeuvre, what with small veins and strenuous objections.

The hours were appalling: we had one night off in three and one short weekend off in three. For the rest of the time we were completely available day and night and worked virtually round the clock, at best getting a few snatched hours of sleep, often interrupted by the telephone.

The first couple of months I went round the hospital with a kind of protective fog round my anxiety. There were so many new things to learn, not to mention such matters as signing death certificates and attending coroners' courts. We were paid for the death certificates, and the convention was that the houseman and registrar split the money between them.

Somehow, in spite of all this, Mrs Rees and I kept going. In truth I think we were only treading water, but she understood the extreme pressures I was under and I was comforted to know that I could see her, even if not very often. I sensed that for her part she was pleased that I'd come this far professionally and was keeping going.

After three months I moved to the general surgical ward, which contained forty beds. There were two housemen, Lindsay Burton and myself. We became friends and supported each other in the various impossibilities of the job. On the consultant's ward round I used to pride myself on not only remembering each patient's name and operation, but also at least a scanty social history. Neville was impressed by this, although I was never to mention that I planned to become a psychiatrist.

One patient I particularly remember was a young man whose symptom had been bleeding from the rectum. He had been misdiagnosed, and when he got to us we discovered he had carcinoma of the rectum. Neville removed this and created a permanent colostomy on his abdomen. He showed great courage, and I often wondered what happened to him. Another patient was an eighty-year-old woman who had a gastric ulcer and who was too frail for a general anaesthetic. One of the surgeons, who was a religious man, decided to operate using a local anaesthetic. This was a deeply unorthodox procedure, but with assistance from Lindsay and myself it was successful.

It was already in my mind that I wanted to become a psychiatrist and also to train as a psychoanalyst. I told Mrs Rees, who promptly dismissed my second aspiration. She explained kindly but firmly that homosexuals couldn't be accepted for training because they wouldn't understand heterosexual development. I was acquiescent as usual, and I didn't enquire whether heterosexual analysts could understand homosexual development. I believe that the thinking behind this was that homosexuals are 'stuck' at an earlier stage of development. Things did change, I believe, and certainly later on I knew analysts who were bisexual; I think that this is the best position for understanding other people's complicated sexual development. On the other hand, bisexuals sometimes have their own difficulties.

While working as a surgical houseman I soon became aware of Gareth Vaughan. He was a charge nurse, and it was clear that he was interested in me – and not only for professional reasons. After a busy day I was sometimes able to relax at night. Gareth would order a late supper, which we ate together. He sometimes also invited the laboratory technician, who later became a celebrated children's author, to join us. Gareth tried to explore my sexual status by various manoeuvres, but I wasn't ready to declare myself, although he was clearly homosexual and was making overtures towards me. Years later, when he'd become a priest and I was a trainee psychiatrist, he visited me in my flat in Swiss Cottage and we went to bed together. He suggested, correctly, that this was the first time I'd had sex with a man of the cloth. He tried to keep in touch, but I was still inhibited and also, I suppose, in some ways snobbish; and I didn't reply.

After six months' surgery I moved to the medical wards. The surgical senior registrar congratulated Lindsay and me on being such excellent housemen. Medicine was much easier than surgery

– for one thing the hours were better – and the job was much more to my taste. I worked for another decent consultant, Dr Norris, and soon became a proficient and reliable junior doctor.

It became possible to have the beginnings of a social life, and, with the anchor of my analysis, which I had more regularly again, I started to explore my homosexual identity. There was a coffee bar near Piccadilly, which had the reputation of having a gay clientele. I went there one evening, with some anxiety, and queued up for coffee beside the fountain in the forecourt. Next to me there was a handsome young man who smiled and was keen to talk. He told me that he'd been an actor and had appeared in a musical called *Wish You Were Here* at the London Casino. However, he'd decided that he would not have a successful stage career and became a salesman. He told me that he was appearing in a leading part in an amateur production of *Kiss Me Kate*, at the Scala theatre. This was of course the scene of my earlier encounter with Kieran Tunney. I didn't make any arrangement to see him again, but I decided to go to the show. Having seen him in it, I daringly wrote him a letter and suggested a meeting. He replied and we arranged to do so outside the Arts Theatre.

He arrived on time and suggested we go to the A & B Club. This was all new territory to me, and we climbed the stairs to some quite elegant premises with some quite elegant younger and older men in them. We had some drinks and he told me that I had 'wicked eyes'. After this we went back to his bed-sitting room in West Hampstead. Although it was clear that he expected a sexual outcome, I was quite ignorant about what moves should be made. The room was partly filled with a double bed, and we sat on the floor looking at his theatrical photographs and press cuttings. It was clear that at some point I was supposed to make a move, but my anxiety and passivity prevented me. Eventually we somehow embraced and got ourselves on to the bed.

He asked me how old I was, and when I said thirty-six there was a slight but obvious physical withdrawal on his part. Soon after this he asked, "Who's going to turn over?" I asked him if anybody had to do so and the answer seemed to be yes. In the end it was me, and he stuck his penis between my legs. It was all quite unsatisfactory, and after it was over we got into the bed. He seemed to be asthmatic and breathed noisily. In the morning I said goodbye and promised to telephone. A few days later I did so and suggested meeting again. He sounded wary and made excuses. I felt greatly rejected and blamed my clumsy performance. Later I discovered that this was a frequent pattern in homosexual relationships: two men meet, go to bed together, exchange telephone numbers the next morning, and often that is the end of it. I had behaved in this way myself, although I didn't fully understand why it should be so.

However, this was not the end of my contact with this person. Years later, when I was familiar with the gay world, I went one evening to a homosexual pub in Earls Court. He was standing there waiting to pick somebody up. After a couple of pints I went up to him and said, "Isn't it Eddie Sutherland?" He looked startled and had no idea who I was. I said we'd met before, to which he replied aggressively, "Have you got a card index?" I never saw him again.

CHAPTER 16

By now I was determined to become a psychiatrist. I was advised that I should take a house job in neurology and then apply to the Institute of Psychiatry at the Maudsley Hospital. My advisor suggested that I approach Dr Ritchie Russell, a well-known neurologist who worked both at the John Radcliffe Hospital in Oxford and also at Stoke Mandeville Hospital in Buckinghamshire. He was welcoming and friendly, and he offered me a six-month job as a senior house officer, which I accepted. As usual I'd not thought enough about my strengths and weaknesses, and I soon realised that I didn't have the intellectual capabilities needed in a neurologist. It was necessary to work out which part of the nervous system was causing the problem, although having done so there seemed to be little one could then do about it.

Dr Russell surrounded himself with bright young men, and I felt out of my depth, though I tried to make myself useful. During my first week a young man on a respirator died. There was an inquest and I had to go to the coroner's court, although I had nothing to do with his care. I prepared a summary of his treatment, which I submitted, but foolishly I didn't keep a copy. When I was questioned by the coroner, I had no notes and was at a loss. "I should remind you that you are an expert witness," the coroner said. I retorted that my notes had not been returned; I complained, and this retrieved the situation to some extent.

My main task, however, was to take part in a research scheme into multiple sclerosis at Stoke Mandeville Hospital. The hypothesis was that patients who had injections of PPD (purified protein derivative) by lumbar puncture would have fewer relapses. I don't recall that there was a control group. I wheeled my trolley round the ward and injected this substance into the patients. I'd been nervous about lumbar punctures, but I found, as with intravenous work, that I became good at it. After the injections, the patients developed high temperatures and had to be watched.

We also admitted patients with other neurological conditions, and my job was to examine them on arrival and make some tentative diagnoses. Ward rounds were usually quite friendly occasions; Dr Russell was friendly, and the second consultant, Charles Whittey, amusing. On one occasion I heard him muttering to himself, "What's the serum – Nescafé?" He also invited me to supper with his elegant wife, and we discussed Sandy Wilson's musical *Valmouth*, which was then running in London. One memorable line we quoted was that of Fenella Fielding playing an elderly lady smitten with a country lad: "I want to spank the white walls of his cottage."

Towards the end of my time at Stoke Mandeville, however, one ward round changed my view of the unit. The usually benign Dr Russell arrived and was obviously deeply upset about something. He questioned me about a number of patients we'd admitted in the past week, and when I was unable to provide appropriate diagnoses he said, "You haven't thought enough about it." The others on the ward round looked shocked, and I was devastated. When my time was up, Dr Russell asked if I would do another six months, but I refused. I knew that neurology wasn't for me, and I knew that he also knew this.

Years later he killed himself in a bizarre way: I read that he'd electrocuted himself while in the bath. He was obviously a complicated man, and I had no idea what really went on inside that usually benign exterior.

CHAPTER 17

I was now unemployed. Two friends moved out of a rented flat in Swiss Cottage and I inherited it. I looked in the *British Medical Journal* each week for possible junior psychiatric jobs and began writing a play. I still had an idea that I could write, but I ignored the basic advice to write about what you know. As a result I wrote a bad play about young heterosexual love, which went straight into a drawer. Unwisely I gave it to Jill and Ken to read; and their lack of enthusiasm was only too clear.

I began again to experiment sexually. I'd only been living in King Henry's Road for a few days when a man driving a motor scooter stopped in the street and introduced himself. I was surprised but flattered, and I agreed to go to supper with him. I'd obviously been spotted as some new talent in the area, and after supper it was clear that bed was going to be our next destination. I sent out negative signals, partly because I wasn't attracted to him and partly because I'd not yet got used to the rapid progress of these encounters. From then on he would acknowledge me frostily as he sailed by on his scooter.

Before long, however, I had a more serious encounter. I was walking down Haverstock Hill one evening when a young man stopped in front of me, bent down and retied his shoelace. I caught up with him and it was clear that he wished to pick me up; and I wanted him to do so. We arranged to go to the pictures a few days later, which we did. Afterwards, we walked to my flat in King Henry's Road, and no doubt we had a few drinks. Next there was the question of bed to be negotiated. Although I was a quick learner, the props were not ideal because, for some reason which I have forgotten, I was sleeping in a narrow camp bed.

It was clear that he liked being penetrated, although his tight arse suggested little practice. I had no experience of anal sex, and lacked the simplest of aids, such as a lubricant. As a result the encounter wasn't a success. But in spite of this we agreed to meet again, and for a while we became regular sexual partners. We developed a technique, which I enjoyed very much; this was being able to feel close to another male, cuddle him and both reach orgasm, preferably simultaneously.

John was a tricky person; there was something permanently cool about him. After a few such encounters he arrived one evening and I embraced him, but then he withdrew, saying, "I'm not sure of my feelings." I felt extremely rejected and used my analytic session the next day to talk about this. By the end of the fifty minutes I'd decided on my reaction: the next time we met I told John that while he was so indecisive I didn't want to see him again. He looked astonished as I let him leave.

I didn't see John again for several weeks, but then I ran into him one day near my house. He obviously wanted to see me again, and, without more ado, we went home and to bed. He never again behaved in this way, although there were other problems. John was highly promiscuous, and I soon learned that I was not the only person to be fitted into his complicated life. Quite soon I abandoned my ideal of having a stable, monogamous relationship and entered with enthusiasm into the promiscuous homosexual world.

John and I settled into a relationship in which he usually visited me or I him on Thursdays, while Saturdays were kept free for separate sexual encounters. On Thursdays we would drink gin and tonic before going to bed. He didn't much enjoy our spending the night together, and when I was in his flat he was inclined to ask if I was staying because if so he would switch the hot water on.

On Saturdays I often went to Primrose Hill. After dark there were scatterings of men on their own, each of them wanting to pick up another male. I quite often 'scored', though I never felt confident about doing so. If I had no luck, I used to walk to Haverstock Hill and do a circular tour along England's Lane, including the public lavatory along the way. Meeting people in lavatories is called 'cottaging' and it was a popular activity. I can still remember the smell of stale urine, which was unpleasant; but the smell was also linked with the pleasurable prospect of picking somebody up.

After some weeks I found two advertisements for a junior psychiatric post. One was at a hospital in Hertfordshire and the other St Clement's Hospital in Bow, East London. I applied for both and accepted the job at the Hertfordshire hospital; but I was then invited to an interview at St Clement's and was keen to go because it was linked to the London Hospital. The senior registrar, Daphne Collins, interviewed me and was keen that I should get the job. The fact that I was having analysis seemed to add to my attractiveness in her eyes, although when she mentioned this to the elderly consultant, Dr Harris, he looked uncertain. Apart from anything else it meant that I wouldn't get to the hospital until 10 a.m. on some days, but Daphne prevailed and I was appointed for six months as a senior house officer.

St Clement's was, in fact, not much to write home about. I was appointed partly to the emergency ward and the rest of my time was to be in the so-called Neurosis Unit. I was also expected to administer ECT, and I remember Daphne's look of dismay when on my first attempt I was so nervous that my hands shook as I gave the intravenous Pentothal.

The emergency ward admitted people who had been sectioned for various reasons – sometimes for violent behaviour. My most celebrated patient was Nancy Cunard, a darling from the 1920s who was rumoured to have had an affair with the Duke of Windsor. I was flattered that she called me David, and I suspect she was confusing me with her royal friend. She was highly manic and kept writing nonsensical words on scraps of paper. After a few days she was transferred elsewhere, and I believe she died fairly soon afterwards.

The Neurosis Unit was unworthy of the name. Daphne ran a patient group and chided me for being so silent. She was an anxious person and needed to keep the conversation flowing, while I said nothing unless I felt able to contribute. In truth, nobody had much idea of what to do with this assortment of non-psychotic patients, which included depressives and those with personality disorders, amongst others. The supposed expert was Miss Pritchard, a psychiatric social worker. She enjoyed being the expert on emotional problems, and the one to whom the staff in their ignorance turned. I refused to do this, and we became enemies as a result. In truth I was flying by the seat of my pants; but, as a colleague once described me, I was a 'green-fingered psychiatrist', and I soon realised that I'd found a career in which I could feel confident. Things came to a head with Miss Pritchard when I ignored her advice (which I'd not asked for) about patients. I was treating one adolescent girl who had an 'hysterical' limp, and Miss Pritchard's advice was to tell her "to put her foot down". I ignored this, although my own treatment was equally mistaken. I knew a hypnotist (also called Black) and he agreed to hypnotise her; after a few sessions, however, one of her arms began to become paralysed and we soon abandoned this unhelpful treatment.

Pat Tooley, who had treated me kindly at the London when I'd broken down as a student, was also a consultant at St Clement's. I was nervous because he knew about my homosexuality, but he greeted me warmly and it was soon obvious that his attitude towards it was more tolerant than my own. Others, however, were not so tolerant; when one of the registrars left (the same medical student with whom I'd travelled to France), he refused to pass on his patients to me because I was "unsuitable father material". He and Miss Pritchard were allies, and I suspect that she was behind this attitude towards my sexuality.

My morale improved, however, towards the end of my six months, when Dr Harris, who was medical superintendent of Claybury Hospital, told me that there was a vacancy for a registrar and that I'd be likely to get the job if I applied. I was flattered, especially because of his earlier reservations about my analysis, and within a few weeks I was making the longer journey to Essex. I learned more about adult psychiatry at Claybury than anywhere else (apart, of course, from my own analysis), and this was due largely to Denis Martin, the man who took over from Dr Harris.

I stayed at Claybury for over two years and moved round various parts of the hospital. Denis was a pioneer of the 'therapeutic community movement', and he was slowly transforming Claybury from a long-stay mental hospital ('bin') into a place where both patients and staff could contribute to better emotional health. The emphasis was on group work, of which there were a number of varieties. My first job was in a 'back ward'. The patients were all women and most had been in the hospital for a good many years. Sister Moreau and I were new brooms, and we decided to change things. Many patients had lost touch with their relatives, and we tried to trace these when possible. We started a weekly magazine, written by the patients, which we circulated throughout the hospital. I subscribed, at the hospital's expense, to a picture-loaning scheme, and I was gently admonished by the hospital administrator for spending his money.

Sister Moreau and I held weekly group meetings, which I think the patients enjoyed. Many were psychotic and had been subjected to one or more lobotomies. Some were talkative, others silent. We might be talking about some topic when there would be a bizarre interruption: for example, one woman announced that she was having an affair with Mantovani, the famous bandleader.

My favourite patient was Miss Page. She was a 'lady' and had been a schoolteacher before having a psychotic breakdown. One day, while I was talking to her in my office, she suddenly sat down in my chair and refused to leave. I entered into the spirit of it and tipped her out of it; we were both highly amused. One thing that puzzled us about Miss Page was that she made frequent visits to the shops in an always unsuccessful attempt to buy shoes. The local shopkeepers were tolerant of our eccentric customers, many of whom no doubt bought their goods. I decided to ask Miss Page why she had such difficulty. The answer was blindingly obvious: it was because her feet didn't belong to her, and this made perfect sense.

At Claybury I met Nina Coltard, who later became a celebrated psychoanalyst. I remember our first meeting: she was sitting by the fireplace in the doctors' sitting room. "I'm having an analysis," she announced, and I took this to be a mark of superiority. We soon became friends, and I talked to her freely about my sexuality. She was a curious mixture, by turns haughty and then lacking in confidence. At that time she was living with a male psychiatrist, and she arrived at Claybury one day with a black eye. She explained that she had fallen against the gas stove, but the truth was that he'd hit her.

For several years we met on Friday evenings. We would either stay in her flat, drink a good deal and eat supper, or perhaps we would go to a restaurant or theatre. At that time she suffered from short-lived depressions, and I never knew from one week to the next in what mood I'd find her. We used to speculate about her 'illness', and she told me that her analyst, Eva Rosenfeld, had said, "You're so talented, but so ill." I believe that Eva was analysed by Freud.

Nina had had a difficult early life. When she was an adolescent during the war, she was evacuated to Cornwall with her younger sister. One evening the telephone rang and Nina answered it. The caller explained that the train on which her parents were travelling to Cornwall had crashed and the casualties were not yet known. A second call explained that both were dead. This had a profound influence on her, though we both speculated that the seeds of disturbance were already inside her before then.

It flattered me that Nina used me as a consultant in her work with patients, and I was probably helpful. She lived a lonely professional life, sitting with patients for many hours a day, although later on she became very important in the political structure of the Institute of Psychoanalysis.

I don't know what she felt for me physically. Though I have a good memory for the generality of our meetings, I cannot recall the discussions which led to our going to bed together, nor indeed the details of the encounter. I have no doubt that I got fairly drunk in order to attempt this unknown and virtually forbidden sexual act, and that it wasn't a success. However, the next morning I left her and walked down the hill to my flat feeling pleased with myself. I had at least made the attempt, although it was never repeated.

Quite late on in our regular meetings I began to hear about an obviously special patient called Jan. Jan had been deeply depressed and had tried to kill herself. Under Nina's care she recovered, and one evening Nina told me that after much careful discussion the analysis had been ended and they were now lovers. I wasn't only shocked by this revelation, but I soon realised that it was to have a profound effect on our own relationship. Nina and I had started going to meditation classes, and Jan began turning up at these. Then she would appear at Nina's flat late in the evening, when we were having supper. It was clear that she was seeking proprietorial rights over her former analyst.

The nature of their relationship became clear when I was with Nina one evening in her flat. Jan was expected, but she failed to

78

arrive. Nina lost control completely, howled and crawled about the floor. I did my best to console her, and I reasoned that Jan had simply been delayed (which was the case), but nothing helped until her lover arrived. This episode starkly revealed Nina's fear of loss, as it presumably reactivated her experience of the loss of her parents.

At some point after this Nina told me that she no longer wanted to see me weekly: she said that this was much too often. I felt extremely rejected, and this was one of the few occasions in my life when I reacted aggressively rather than passively. Although we were due to meet the following week I didn't arrive, and this in turn upset Nina. When we did meet again we had a furious row, and we didn't see each other again for some time. Eventually, however, and passive as ever, I settled for seeing her about twice a year, for such things as birthday outings. Our relationship was still important to me, although I never again trusted her completely.

Nina's final years were unhappy. She moved from Hampstead to Bedfordshire in semi-retirement. By then she had acquired a group of woman friends to whom she gave money or property. Physically she was deteriorating. Although she had become a very moderate drinker she still smoked heavily and became breathless on exertion. She perforated a duodenal ulcer, which was repaired, and she also had osteoporosis.

The last time I saw her she had quite visibly changed. Her face was puffy and she seemed miserable. She had been told to give up smoking, which she was trying unsuccessfully to do. We discussed her state. I was myself bereaved at the time (having lost my long-term partner, Keith) and it seemed to me that in some curious way giving up smoking was perhaps an outward sign of her permanent internal bereavement. Whatever the truth of this, I never saw her again: she killed herself with an overdose a few months later.

CHAPTER 18

At Claybury there was a rota for duty psychiatrists at night. One registrar stayed until 6 p.m. and the other slept at the hospital. One evening, when I was on night duty and my friend Roland Berry was on until 6 p.m., we were in adjoining cubicles admitting two new woman patients. He had a date and was in a hurry. Through the curtain I heard him say soothingly, "Now, madam, just relax," then again in a slightly peremptory way, "Just please relax," and finally, "Come along, madam – you must relax!"

The unfortunate lady was stung into replying, "But that's why I've come into hospital – because I can't relax."

My favourite posting was to the Neurosis Unit. This was Denis's special unit and was largely run along group lines. There was a daily general morning meeting which all patients and staff attended, and this was followed by various smaller groups, led by either the psychiatric nurses or occupational therapists. It was difficult to know how much good we did, but at least some of the patients trusted their group enough to explore hidden and therefore frightening emotions and to discover that the world didn't end and that the group still accepted them.

During my time at Claybury I became close to Denis. He wasn't so much older than I was, but I looked up to him as a senior male. He lived in a house in the grounds of the hospital with his wife and three daughters. I was usually invited to Sunday lunch when on weekend duty, and I sensed that Denis welcomed my male company.

He was an extremely complicated and sensitive man, and I valued his ability to be silent and to take seriously any contribution made in a group discussion. Some time after I left the hospital I heard that he was ill. At first it appeared that he'd developed severe eczema, but it soon became clear that he'd also become severely depressed. I think there was some feeling that for a senior psychiatrist to be depressed was something a bit shameful. With my own history, I didn't share this view! Another difficulty was which senior psychiatrist could treat another senior psychiatrist? I don't know the details, but I believe that he saw several eminent people who couldn't help him much. I visited him at the London Hospital. He was in a severely regressed state, lying on his side, and, as I recall, not speaking. I don't know what treatments were tried, but eventually he was judged well enough to go back to Claybury on a trial basis. It wasn't a success, and he retired to a small house nearby.

Nina and I visited him and his wife, Jean. It was as if the life force had left him. He no longer seemed depressed exactly, but feeble. His eczema was still bad and he was developing cataracts. One action of his somehow summed up to me his state of mind: when I went to the bathroom he warned me that there was something wrong with the washbasin. Perhaps there wasn't a plug or maybe the tap didn't work – whatever it was, no attempt had been made to repair it. This was the last time that I saw him; he died soon afterwards.

CHAPTER 19

When it was time to leave Claybury, I had to decide what to do next. I heard that there was a vacancy for a registrar at the Child Guidance Training Centre in Hampstead, and I decided to apply. The medical director was a cool, rather frosty analyst called Susanna Davidson, and she questioned me closely about why I wanted experience in child psychiatry. I've no idea what I replied, but I was left feeling that I was very much wanting. However, the day was saved when I was interviewed by a second consultant, Piers Debenham. He was laid-back, and a charming man. When I told him my analyst was Jean Rees, he chortled and told me that she had been the psychiatric social worker there. This was obviously somewhat incestuous, but it did the trick and I got the job.

In truth the clinic was living on past glories and offered a very poor training. There were four consultants: Susanna Davidson, Piers Debenham, Margaret Collins and a recently appointed one, Lionel Hersov. Lionel was a consultant of the new guard, and he believed in such things as research and evidence. There was also a senior psychologist, Nora Gibbs, and a child psychotherapist, Jess Guthrie, who it turned out lived in the basement flat of my analyst's now rather swanky house in St John's Wood.

On my first morning I arrived and nervously introduced myself to Margaret Collins: "I'm Michael Black."

"I know," she said.

Margaret was a Jungian as indeed my analyst (at least technically) was. She said that I must be invited to some Jungian professional meetings, but she must have subsequently heard that I was on the panel and I never had an invitation.

Psychiatric social workers (PSWs) were the most powerful professional group at the centre, and they really ran the place. There was a case conference each week, at the conclusion of which the treatment almost invariably offered was for the PSW to see the mother and the psychiatrist to see the child for weekly sessions. Fathers didn't get a look in. The junior doctors called each other by first names, but otherwise the psychiatrists were called Doctor and the PSWs called Miss. The juniors had seminars from the psychiatrists, the senior psychologists and the child psychotherapist. The pace was leisurely, but, as the training model was outdated, much of our time could have been used more constructively. For example, there was no training in paediatrics, and no mention of behaviour-modification techniques and family therapy.

After about a year the senior registrar decided to leave to return to Ireland and write novels. He had been a somewhat subversive influence on our group. There was now a vacancy for the senior post and I was encouraged to apply. The appointments committee, a formidable group of senior consultants, interviewed me. I was no good at interviews because I became anxious and my low self-esteem prevented me from demonstrating my strengths. There was another candidate, Naomi Richman – someone with an academic background, which I didn't possess. However, consultants from the clinic wanted me and I was appointed.

When I was called back into the room, the chairman said, "There is just one thing: we are sorry that you aren't married."

I tried to make a joke of it and said, "I'll have to do something about it," but in fact this was something of a body blow, and as a result I never felt really comfortable in my position as senior registrar.

Despite this I was enthusiastic about my job. I took on a heavy caseload and organised the junior psychiatrists' training programme.

CHAPTER 20

My private life was still complicated. John and I continued our open relationship, and one day he told me he had applied for training in landscape architecture in the USA. He asked me whether I would give him a reference. Passive as ever, I agreed, although I felt devastated. On the day that he left, we went to a gay pub and, after he had gone, I took some amphetamine.

I was still promiscuous, and one evening I eyed a young man in the lift at Belsize Park Underground Station; he eyed back and took me to his bed-sitting room nearby. His name was William, and he said he hated living there and he hated his job in a publishing firm. Soon afterwards he visited me in my flat. I had misgivings about my promiscuous state, and I usually tried to get to know somebody only if I thought he might become a friend. William sat on the arm of my easy chair and said, "I hope we shall not have to wait long." Indeed we didn't! We embarked on a short-lived, passionate sexual affair. William ended this quite abruptly, but not before he'd given his landlord notice and moved into my spare room. He was a highly intelligent, disturbed Welshman, an only child from the Rhondda Valley. On the face of it we were not a good couple: I resented his dependence on me when I was so needy myself. But, as I now realise, there was part of me that liked relating to young and uncertain males and helping them to develop their lives. Another problem about living with another man was admitting this to other people. I forbade him to answer the telephone and was dismayed one day when he visited me at the clinic.

One Saturday evening he took me to visit Marian Dutter. She was an alcoholic lady who gave 'parties' for gay men. In those days male homosexuality was still illegal, and there were few opportunities for meeting apart from the anonymity of such places as Hampstead Heath and public lavatories. I have no idea why she felt moved to offer what was a social service. It wasn't only an opportunity to get drunk; it was also an opportunity to pick somebody up.

I was ill at ease, but after several glasses of wine I began talking to a young American called C. D. He invited me back to his flat, gave me supper and took me to bed. The next day he suggested we meet and he came to my flat in Swiss Cottage. He interested me greatly because he seemed to know everybody in show business. He was a composer, and he later became celebrated for composing scores for television and music to accompany restored silent films. He also did a good deal of conducting. There was, however, a fly in the ointment: he told me that he was in therapy with a friend of mine, an ex-colleague, and I was dismayed that I had sexual contact with one of his patients. Looking back, I don't suppose he would have minded, although I never discussed it with him. I quickly distanced myself from C. D., but not before he'd invited me to have supper with him at a restaurant at the far end (from me) of the No. 31 bus route. I can only remember wanting to get away and our journey back on the bus to North London, when he told me that whenever he wanted to get close to somebody they went away. My guilt about C. D. was probably needless because he went on to have a successful and lucrative career and married an actress.

I was still ashamed of my sexuality and stopped my visits to the local gay pub in Hampstead altogether when I discovered that one of the secretaries at the clinic was working in the evenings for the coffee bar next door. There was little possibility that she would see me, but it was enough to make me give up this important part of my life. Instead I was to visit the 'cottages' in Haverstock Hill and Primrose Hill. During this period I picked up a considerable number of young men. I don't recall their names, although I recall some of the encounters. There was a young man who sat beside me on a bench; he asked me if I wanted a 'rub-up', explaining that his penis was small and brown. I persuaded him to come back to my flat, but this wasn't what he wanted. He departed without sex, but with a copy of James Baldwin's *Giovanni's Room*.

Another young man, George, was quite willing to come home with me, though neither he nor I wanted to prolong the relationship. I was disconcerted, to put it mildly, when I met him at the entrance to the Tavistock clinic. I'd joined a professional course and he a patient group.

I encountered a young black man on Haverstock Hill while drunk. We went to a secluded spot, and with practised ease he buggered me before departing. By the next morning I was extremely anxious and consulted a venereologist. Fortunately the results were negative. I knew the risks I was taking, but when drunk I temporarily accepted them.

One evening I went to the Stockpot Restaurant in the West End, where I met a young American and invited him home. He told me that he'd developed gonorrhoea in Amsterdam and had been cured with penicillin; however, the next day he telephoned to say that the discharge had come back and also that the immigration authorities had deemed him an undesirable alien. This encounter led to another trip to the venereologist (the results were again negative), and it became increasingly clear that I was leading an unsatisfactory and potentially dangerous lifestyle.

My domestic life was also running into trouble. Eton College, who owned my flat, were seeking to knock our houses down and build more profitable new ones. I took fright and moved to the next road, to a flat rented by a colleague who was going back to the United States. I kept my tenancy in King Henry's Road and rented it to two young men. Another difficulty was that my sister and brother-in-law left Hampstead for Cornwall; this meant that strong support was removed. These changes affected me greatly and, combined with the unsatisfactory nature of the clinic, led to a falling-off in my work. I took on fewer new patients, went home at lunchtime, drank gin and Vermouth and ate Wiener schnitzel (to my shame) at a local restaurant.

Without realising it at first I was becoming depressed again. Once Dr Davidson, during my supervision, asked me what further training I needed. I took this to mean that the clinic had had enough of me as a senior registrar. In addition I was treading water in my analysis. I began increasingly to feel that I was ill fitted to being a child psychiatrist, and I felt that I should look for work which was less concerned with emotions. I saw an advertisement for a job as a research assistant in social medicine at Guy's Hospital, and I decided to apply. At my interview I was obviously regarded as something of a catch, and I was appointed at £2,000 a year. This was an extremely foolish career move. I was only eighteen months into a three-year contract with the NHS, which would certainly have led to a well-paid consultancy post. My new job was paid for with a research grant, which could end abruptly. However, I was determined to sabotage my professional chances: I broke my NHS contract by only giving six weeks' notice instead of three months', and I was rightly lectured by the health administrator. "We would have looked after you," he said reprovingly.

My leaving party was a formality; people said nice things, but the reality was that I was a failure and they knew it. One person who showed concern was Betty Tamblyn. She was one of the younger PSWs and was training to be a psychoanalyst. She came to my room and made it clear that she'd picked up my deepening depression. She told me that she'd wanted to study medicine but had been unable to do so, and she said how disappointed she'd been at the time. This was supportive, although it did nothing to change my situation.

I decided to end my analysis. I'd already missed one session and felt that Mrs Rees disapproved of my behaviour. I cannot remember our discussion about this, although I suspect that Mrs Rees may have been relieved that this 'oh, so promising' patient had proved too resistant to benefit much from her work.

Looking back I can see that I was becoming isolated in several ways from my home, from Jill and Ken, from child psychiatry and from my analyst. These were all major losses. At the clinic I went through the motions, while at the hospital I tried to keep afloat. I look back at this experience as a nightmare; I knew within days that I'd made a terrible mistake. I was mixing with academics and I had no aptitude for the work.

My job was to prepare a questionnaire with which I would then interview general practitioners on their views about attaching health visitors to their practices. In my office I sat with little idea of what to do. I found reading difficult, and I was prescribed glasses. I was forty-four years old and in despair; there was a dream-like quality to my life.

Peter Draper, the senior researcher, realised that I was isolated and invited me to play squash; he meant well, but this offer didn't meet my need. A more sensitive staff member was Gwynn Morris. She and Peter didn't get on, and I began to think that one reason the unit had hired a psychiatrist was to bring some harmony to the group. Gwynn understood that I was floundering, and tactfully gave me hints about how to design a questionnaire. By degrees I managed to produce something presentable, although one less tactful staff member commented that I couldn't make decisions.

The lease on my flat ran out, and William and I had to move. Jill and Ken had bought a little house in the Highgate area, and they offered it to us on a temporary basis. William and I were both unhappy in our different ways and took it out on each other. We had a serious quarrel and I slapped his face. William decided to leave and I was devastated. However, it was for the best, because as soon as we separated we became and remained steadfast friends. Indeed, when he was training to be a teacher, he came to live with me in Gayton Road and this arrangement was a great success.

It was while I was with William that one day the phone rang and it was Vera telling me she had found Harry dead in bed. I burst into tears and, as soon as I could, I caught the train to Sidmouth to meet her. She said to me that when she found Harry dead she asked him to "please, come back". I rang Peter and told him what had happened. Later we went to the funeral.

I wrote to my analyst asking to be taken back, and I went to see her. I thought that she was perhaps irritated by my return, as she had (in her own words) given away my times and had to fit me in as best she could. What neither of us could have realised was that this was the breakthrough that my analysis needed. I sat on the couch and began to cry; she sat next to me and held my hand. The analysis had begun.

Jock Anderson, who ran the research unit, was patient with me; he and I both knew that we'd made a mistake, but he put up with my flounderings until a useable questionnaire emerged. Guy's seemed unendurable and I asked Denis Martin what to do. He said that I should stay for a year, as anything less would look odd on a CV.

I accepted his advice, but when a part-time locum job was offered to me at Uxbridge Child Guidance Clinic, I accepted. This meant I divided my time between Guy's and Uxbridge. I took my questionnaire to GPs for three days a week and went to Uxbridge for two. Within days of working in the clinic, I realised that I did have a vocation and this was work that I could do well.

By this time I'd moved from Jill's house to a basement room in Swiss Cottage. It was dark and isolated, but it suited my depressed mood. One day, however, I was walking from the Underground station to College Crescent when something inside me shifted. I no longer felt the despair; I suddenly realised that my life might have prospects after all. After a few weeks the Uxbridge job was advertised and I applied.

Jock continued to be understanding, and he agreed to be a referee. The clinic staff wanted me, but in the wings there was a senior registrar candidate, and he had already taken a long time in his search for a consultancy. As usual, at the selection committee I performed badly, and I remember one member saying incredulously, "You've only been a locum for six weeks." The other senior registrar was appointed and I began a round of unsuccessful job interviews. I must have been seen as an odd fish (as indeed I was) and a maverick. After several of these, the NHS Administrator told me that there was a vacancy at a child-guidance clinic in Bedford, and there was a good chance that I would be appointed. This wasn't a compliment: the clinic was a notoriously arid place to work and had had difficulty in recruiting child psychiatrists.

I talked it over with Nina and she was blunt: "Apply for it," she said, "otherwise you'll have to leave London."

Whilst still applying I took a job in this clinic as a part-time locum consultant and applied for the full-time job when it was advertised.

There was a snag: the health authority wanted someone who lived locally. I was determined to stay in London and commute. The job description specified that the applicant had to live within ten miles of the clinic. I took a gamble and refused to apply unless this stipulation was removed. They obviously wanted me, and my blackmail worked; the job was re-advertised without this restriction, and I was appointed. No questions were asked about where I lived and although I made up an inaccurate answer about a proposed revision of the NHS (which I had not read) nobody seemed to mind too much. As a celebration, William and I, together with two other friends, drove to the south of France for a holiday. Things were looking up!

On a Saturday evening in July 1967 I took the Underground from Swiss Cottage to Leicester Square in order to go to the Salisbury public house. I sat down on one of the plush velvet seats. Beside me was Keith, the person with whom I was to share the next twenty-five years of my life.

Chapter on Keith

Perhaps the most harrowing episode of my life was when one day in 1993 the phone rang and I heard the voice of Keith, the person with whom I had shared the past twenty-five years of my life. He sounded strange, and I knew something was wrong. In panic I rang Ken, my brother-in-law, and together we raced to Keith's flat in Tufnell Park. When I got through the door I found him dead.

I feel as though since that time I have never quite got over the shock – that I've been grieving for Keith ever since. Grief, I think, changes its shape over time, but there is not a day goes by when I don't think about him. In my flat here in Hampstead I can see the leaf-table he used to own, his sofa, and his paintings that hang on the wall. I didn't ever know that he was so ill, as he didn't talk about it, and I often feel the guilt of not picking up on it.

I remember my sister Jill asking me, shortly after his death, "Is it too terrible?"

"Yes," I replied, "it is."

So, I will go back to the day I met Keith. When that day I sat down on a bench in the Salisbury public house, and noticed the Jamaican man sitting next to me, I knew that here was someone who was going to be important in my life. I had picked people up in the past in pubs, but I knew instinctively that this would be different – that it mattered.

We began seeing each other straight away, but though we were together for twenty-five years we never actually lived together. Nevertheless, our relationship was very harmonious and we very rarely rowed. I always assumed that he was a little younger than

I was, but when he died I discovered he was, in fact, a few months older.

When we first met, Keith was working for the BBC. Later, he took a job at Simpson's, the department store in Piccadilly. He used to supervise the unloading of supply lorries at the back of the store.

Keith had no family in England, but he had aunts and cousins back in Jamaica. His mother had died when he was four years old, and his father had taken off shortly afterwards. His family were very poor, as I discovered on our trip to visit them, and throughout our time together we would send them money. On this trip, we visited the house Keith had lived in when growing up with his aunts. He had had to share a room with one of them. He had a younger brother, and I remember Keith giving him a pair of shoes. We went on a trip with him, and we were shown his school building. It was harrowing for me to see the poverty his family lived in.

We went on several other trips abroad. Those which come to mind include one to Amsterdam, where we stayed in a village outside the city. Keith was especially delighted to meet a woman who dressed up as Mae West (whom he adored). We booked into an awful gay hotel, where the men were over the top and rather ludicrous. We found ourselves another hotel, which was better, but I contracted food poisoning and was ill for three days. I remember visiting Anne Frank House on our visit.

Another trip was to Moscow, which included a tour of the Kremlin. My memory is, in the main, of unfriendliness. We also took a flight to Leningrad, and on to Murmansk, where we were welcomed at the university – apparently they received few visitors there. I recall a rather boozy dinner.

An incident I remember well from the 1960s was standing with Keith in a shop doorway in Golders Green counting cars stopping at the McDonald's opposite to get takeaways. The purpose of this exercise was to gather information to present to the council, as Keith and I were fighting the opening of a McDonald's in Hampstead – the plan was to open one in an existing shop without getting planning permission. The streets in Hampstead were too narrow, we thought, to allow for the extra traffic this would create, and we believed it would have a bad effect on the area. We won our case and McDonald's was refused permission. (Years later they took over an existing Wimpey, where they still are.) Our fight generated rather a lot of interest, and we received many phone calls congratulating us.

Keith was a very private person, and it was only after his death, through talking on the phone with his cousin in New York, Miss Philips, that I discovered he came to England because of being in the air force. Keith was very calm and very loving; his effect on me was often to calm me down. He loved classical music (I, on the other hand, never really had much of an interest), and he was especially fond of Rossini. He kept a box of classical records, neatly labelled. He loved to go to Sadler's Wells to hear concerts. We would often go to the theatre together. He was also something of an artist, and he loved to paint.

I remember Keith's pleasure when I got my maisonette in Hampstead, where he visited me for twenty-five years, and where I still live. I had got the money together for the deposit, partly with the help of my father. It also helped that I didn't have to pay my financial adviser – he regarded it as payment enough that I gave him advice regarding his son, who had a problem controlling the passing of water. On hearing the good news about getting the house, I met up with Keith at a theatre, where a friend of his was appearing in *Half a Sixpence*. He was so pleased.

Keith was adored by my family, and I remember his first introduction to them. It was a visit to Jill and Ken's home in Muswell Hill. I pushed him through the front door ahead of me. They took to him straight away.

My mother adored him. At one point, in fact, I had to put my foot down and insist that Keith's visits to her had to include me, as she seemed to want him all to herself. (She had often tried to 'steal' my friends. I am put in mind of a quote by Lorna Luft, Judy Garland's daughter: "She was the best mother that she knew how to be.") When Vera died, Keith and I attended her funeral together, and her ashes were buried next to her mother's grave in Highgate Cemetery. It was a modest grave, set back from the road, and the ceremony was humanist (reflecting my inclination at the time). I recall us throwing plants – ferns, I think – on to the grave. It was Jill who informed me of Vera's death: she met me in Highgate Wood, looking strangely like Mother – which she never had before – and told me she had passed away in her sleep in her nursing home in Totteridge. I have to confess to feeling a great relief on her passing.

Shortly after Keith's passing, I was taken off on holiday by my friend Marion, a psychologist I had met at Bedford. Doubtless she had my best interests at heart: she was trying to relieve me of my grief. She drove us down to the south of France, where she had friends. I remember drinking a fair amount on this trip, though it didn't help. We actually fell out rather badly over my wanting to have a drink before breakfast – something she disapproved of. I appreciate that she wanted to help, but the trip didn't quite have the desired effect.

Keith once said to me, "You're the best thing that ever happened to me." Without doubt, I could say the same of him.